D0112075

In the Birch Woods of Belarus: A Partisan's Revenge

By *Sidney Simon*

With Maryann McLoughlin, Ph.D.
Edited by Rosalie Simon and Maryann McLoughlin, Ph.D.

A Project of The Richard Stockton College of New Jersey
Holocaust Resource Center and Graphics Prodcution

PUBLISHING

Margate, New Jersey

Copyright © 2009 by Sidney Simon and Maryann McLoughlin, Ph.D.
All rights reserved. No part of this book may be used or reproduced in any
manner, electronic or mechanical, including photocopying, recording or by
any information storage and retrieval system, or otherwise, without written
permission from the publisher.

Published by:
  ComteQ Publishing
  A division of ComteQ Communications, LLC
  P.O. Box 3046
  Margate, New Jersey 08402
  609-487-9000 • Fax 609-487-9099
  Email: publisher@ComteQcom.com
  Website: www.ComteQpublishing.com

ISBN 978-1-935232-00-1
Library of Congress Control Number: 2008943860

Book and cover design by Gary D. Schenck
Back cover photo by Ryan Schocklin

Printed in the United States of America
10 9 8 7 6 5 4 3 2 1

*In memory of
my brother, Mojshe*

After Treblinka
And the spezialkommando
Who tore a child with bare hands
Before its mother in Warsaw
We see differently.

— *"How We See,"* Edward Bond

Acknowledgements

I owe my utmost gratitude and appreciation to Dr. Maryann McLoughlin, from the Holocaust Resource Center of Richard Stockton College, for her many hours of time and patience helping me to write my book. This project would have been impossible without her assistance.

I wish to thank not only Maryann but also Gail Rosenthal of the Holocaust Resource Center, who was the driving force behind the "Writing as Witness" Program. The survivors benefit greatly from all the programs she has designed for them. I want to thank, too, the Dean of General Studies, G. Jan Colijn, who guides the Holocaust Resource Center and all its projects. President Herman Saatkamp is appreciated for his support of the center and its publication projects.

I also thank Stockton's Graphics Production, in particular, Julie Bowen who directs the department, as well as Gary Schenck for the creative cover and book design and Ryan Schocklin for the author photograph.

The book would never have been completed without the assistance of my wife, Rosalie, my partner and friend for over fifty-six years, who listened to and commented on the many versions of the text. She is my beloved.

Sidney (Shimen) Simon
November 2008

Table of Contents

Rosalie's Preface

I feel honored that I have the opportunity to write about my husband, Sidney Simon, to whom I have been married for fifty-six years. Sidney and I are both Holocaust survivors. We both came to the United States at the end of 1949, with literally only the clothes on our backs. Sidney came from a Displaced Persons (DP) Camp in Austria, and I came from Czechoslovakia.

We met in Baltimore, Maryland, in 1950, while attending night school to learn the English language. We dated for two years before we decided to build a life together in this country. We were married on June 1, 1952, in Sidney's parents' home. We had a very small wedding. Sidney's mom prepared some food. We had no wedding album and no honeymoon. Sidney went to work the next day. He knew he had to provide for the family. He worked many long hours, exceedingly hard, trying a build up a scrap metal business. Every night he came home soaked in sweat, totally exhausted from lifting the heavy barrels of metal that he had picked up from various machine shops. These were tough times, but eventually the business started to grow and Sidney began to make a very nice living.

We moved to the Atlantic City area in 1954. Sidney had to give up his scrap metal business, which was still profitable, because it became too difficult to travel back and forth to Baltimore. After some other business ventures that he has written about in his memoir, Sidney started to buy and develop land, remaining in land developing until retirement.

One of Sidney's many virtues, which served him well in both his personal and professional life and I believe contributed to his success, was that when dealing with people, he conducted himself with high moral and ethical standards. In addition, in his own quiet way, he helped many people in need and generously supported many charities.

Over the years, he has worked for his community, for Israel, and for the United States. He has been honored often: The Jerusalem Award for Outstanding Service and Leadership—1970; The New Life Award for the Support of Israel—1991; Who's Who among Executives and Professionals—1994-1995; Tribute from the Federation of Jewish Agencies; Scroll of Honor from the Hebrew Academy; and in the 80s, the New Jersey General Assembly Award for Support of the State of Israel and the Cause of Jewish Freedom.

Sidney frequently speaks of what he went through during the Holocaust. The events he experienced in the past are as vivid for him today as they were over sixty-seven years ago. Indeed, it is most difficult for him to let go of the past. The memories are still very painful. Yet no matter how painful the memories are, Sidney is able to live in the present—with optimism and peace.

Sidney recognizes and appreciates that he has been blessed with many gifts.

We are blessed with three wonderful children: Mitchell, Ruthie, and William (Billy), two lovely daughters-in-law: Debbie and Jody, and five grandchildren: Jared, Matthew, Daniel, Erik, and Raegan Aliya, who have brought us much joy. We are proud of each and every one of them.

I consider myself very lucky to have survived the Holocaust and I am grateful to have Sidney as my life's partner. Hopefully, with G-d's blessing, we will have many more years together.

I encouraged Sidney to write his memoir so that he would leave behind for our children, our grandchildren, and future generations, his legacy, his tragic story of what occurred during the Nazi Regime.

Rosalie Simon
November 2008

Genealogy
Simon (Shimenovich) Family

Samuel m Czerna
Mojshe
b. 1923
d. 1942

Katie   m   Isaac   m   Joe   Charlotte
b. 1924   Zachary
d. 1978   Debbie

Sidney   **m 1952**   **Rosalie Lebovic**
b. 8-15-1925   b. 7-25-1931
Mitchell m Debbie 1977   Jared, Matthew, Danny
b.1953

Ruthie   Erik
b. 1956

William m Jody 2005   Raegan Aliya
b. 1967

Richard m Betty   Marsha
b. 1926   Jake
d. 2005   Renee
                            Valeria

Ida m Shunek   Lillian
b. 1929   Jamie
                            Marilyn

Maps of Poland and Belarus

Post WWI to 1939

Belitze is 30 kilometers from Lida (circled). lonelyplanet.org

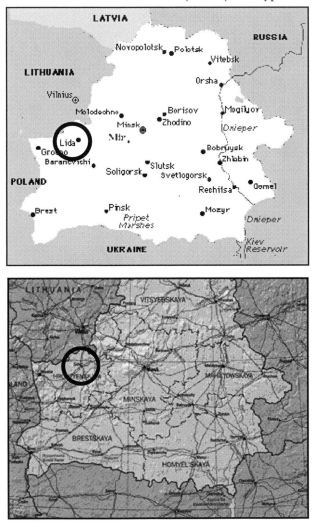

Post WWI to 1939
Belarus 1939-1941, Lida circled
commons.wikimedia.org

Contemporary Map of Belarus cia.gov
Lida indicated with a circle

Chapter One
Belitze, Poland

I was born in Belitze, Poland (thirty kilometers from Lida), founded in the 1300s. Before World War I, when the district had been annexed by Czarist Russia, a number of Jewish families had left Belitze because of poverty and antisemitism. Many immigrated to the United States. After World War I (1914-1918), Belitze, formerly of Belarus, became a part of Poland and conditions improved somewhat.[1] However, by 1939, Belitze was still only a small town; the total population was 1800 and of this number 600 were Jews. (Museum of the Jewish Diaspora)

Belitze is on the Neman River, a large river that runs through Lithuania, Belarus (which some call White Russia), and into Germany.[2] A bridge over the Neman was our connection to many other towns.

Logging was a big industry in the Belitze area. The logs were shipped down the Neman River from the forests of Belarus and Russia. The trees were bound together like rafts and then sent to Germany. On these log rafts were huts where the loggers kept their supplies and clothes and sheltered from the rain and sun. On these rafts, they often built fires, in little portable cast iron stoves, to cook their food. As a child I would often sneak unto these huge rafts until the crew members noticed me. Then I would jump into the river and swim to shore.

The town of Belitze profited from these loggers. Very often they would stop and buy all kinds of products, such as food and liquor for their journey. They were a rough bunch of people; they used to come in the middle of the night and pound on our door demanding that my father open the restaurant so they could buy liquor. My father ignored them, so then they would leave.

The people of Belitze speak a number of languages: Belarusian, some Polish (the language of education was Polish), and some Russian. The Jews also spoke Yiddish and learned Hebrew in religious school.

My ancestors had lived in the Belitze area for generations. My father, Samuel Shimenovich, owned a restaurant and a liquor store. Although Jews by law were forbidden to have liquor licenses and only a volunteer in the Polish army during World War I could get a license, my father had an arrangement with an older man he knew named Bogotki, who could get a license, and so they did.[3] Everyone

from Belitze and the towns all around Belitze knew my father. Often they wanted vodka—sometimes for themselves, sometimes for a wedding. My father would give it to them on credit—with a handshake. They called him "King of Liquor."

My mother, Czerna, was a very good, hard-working woman who helped my father and who even had her own business. She would buy shoes and boots and sell them. My mother had converted one of the rooms in our house into a shoe store with a separate entrance facing the street. In the winter the boots were thick, knitted, woolen boots. My mother had a housekeeper/nanny, Jenka, who had helped to raise all five of the children: three boys, Mojshe (b. 1923), Shimen (Sidney)(b. 1925), Richard (b. 1926), and two girls, Katie (b. 1924) and Ida (b. 1929). We lived very comfortably.

My mother was a virtuous and kind woman. I remember that she forgave the housekeeper for both minor and serious mistakes. The housekeeper had an uncle in another village and he would come to our house on a sled. He manipulated our housekeeper and pressured her until she would help him by stealing some of my mother's shoes and boots. Under the straw in the sled, he would conceal these shoes and boots that had been taken from my mother's shelves.

My mother noticed that her stock of shoes and boots was disappearing, so she told my father. My father suspected that the uncle was the thief; therefore, he asked his friend who was in the police to go with him to search the uncle's house. I, too, went with them. When they went to the uncle's house, they found the shoes that the uncle had been selling little by little. The police told my father that they were going to lock up Jenka, the housekeeper. My father reluctantly agreed. My mother, however, said to my father, "How can you do this? She has raised our children and been with us for a long time." Jenka continued as our housekeeper, and my mother trusted that she would not steal again. I saw all of this because I was very attached to my father, following him everywhere.

I was born on August 15, 1925.[4] I had a happy childhood. I remember swimming in the River Neman. When I was five, my father took me into the river on his back and swam with me for a while. When we were a distance from shore, he dropped me off his back. I had to struggle until I learned how to swim. I learned! I also loved to fish, especially with my older brother, Mojshe.

I helped around the house. My chores were in the garden and the restaurant. We didn't have running water so I used to carry water in buckets from a nearby well. We used the water in the house and in the garden. In the restaurant I would clean the wooden tables.

I had time, too, to play with my friends in the woods. We would climb trees and pick wild fruit and berries.

Chapter Two

School Days

I went to public school and also to religious school. I first went to a Hebrew elementary school. I often got into mischief in the Hebrew School, especially in Polish class. The teacher, Civia, was a Polish Jew who spoke very good Polish. She and my cousin, the Hebrew teacher, Hirshe Leizer, fell in love and eventually married. His house and ours were next door to one another. I liked him although he teased me. One day I saw him smoking a cigarette and I asked him for one. He said, "I'll give you the cigarette when the dark ring disappears," meaning that I would not get any of the cigarette because when the dark ring disappeared the cigarette was finished. Another time he asked me if I liked Civia. I said, "No!" He told me that he might marry her. I said, "That is bad; she is no good." They married anyway.

In class Civia carried a ruler and that ruler kept my hands swollen. Just being in her class made me hate school. I thought often about how to get back at her. When I was eight or nine, I came up with this plan: teachers kept their chalk in a wooden box the size of a matchbox. After school I was at my uncle's bakery, and he showed me tiny, just born mice. They didn't yet have fur. Without his knowledge, I took a mouse to school early one morning, and I replaced the chalk with the little mouse. That day Civia was walking around the classroom with the box in her hand. Then when she was ready to write on the blackboard, she reached into the chalk box and grabbed the mouse; she jumped almost to the ceiling. She called me right away: "Shimenovitch, come here." She hit me with the ruler many times, gave me detention in the principal's office, and made me do a lot of work, writing something over and over. In this office the principal kept the supplies, such as ink. I decided to take a break from writing. I made the blackboard greasy so it could not be written on. Then I poured out half the ink and diluted it. Next day when a child needed ink, the ink wouldn't write.

Another time the teacher caught me and some other boys smoking. We didn't have regular tobacco; therefore, we picked dried leaves, especially cherry leaves for their flavor, and used newspaper to make the cigarettes. The synagogue was near the school, so we ran to the synagogue and smoked inside. A rabbi, also my Hebrew teacher, found out and punished us. We had to do a ton of extra work in the office.

In Hebrew School we had pen pals from Palestine. We dried flowers of Belarus and sent these to Palestine and our pen pals sent us flowers from Palestine.

At the Hebrew School they didn't have teachers for the higher grades, so when I was older I transferred to public school. I switched to a Polish school where there were White Russians, Polish, and Jewish children. We were four or five Jewish girls and five Jewish boys. The girls and boys were separated in the school. The boys wore a cap with a brim that had metal trim and a Polish eagle insignia. The girls mixed with the non-Jewish girls, sitting next to them. The five Jewish boys sat in assigned seats—on one bench in the back. This was always our seat. The boys did not mix—the non-Jewish boys didn't want anything to do with us. Mostly they tormented us, fighting with us at school.

Every morning—every single morning!—the non-Jewish boys stood on benches on both sides of the door and when we five came in they would hit us with the pieces of metal from their caps. We had to take it. We had told the teacher, but he did nothing. He said he would take care of it, but he never did.

One morning we said, "We have to do something about them." We couldn't take it any more. So we decided to take clubs and put them up our sleeves. When we got to the door, we ran in and quickly turned right around and hit them with the sticks. Boys and girls scattered, running to the huge windows to exit. I grabbed one boy, pulling him back from the window, and the eagle, the symbol of Poland, fell off his hat.

These boys went to the principal crying. Then the principal pulled all the Jewish boys to the front of the room. He lined us up in front of the blackboard and asked, "What happened?" We told him, "We couldn't take it any longer. Every morning they hit us." The principal didn't care about us. He was angry that we had fought back and that I had knocked the Polish eagle off the boy's cap. He felt I was unpatriotic. He beat us with a huge club; the club was broken on our bodies. He took me and another guy aside and gave us a letter to take to another school—the higher grades were in this school. The letter was written in Latin so we couldn't read it. This teacher in the higher grade said, "I'll take care of you guys. Stay here all afternoon." He put us on a bench in the rear of the

room. Afterward we ran home. Our parents did not come to school to complain; it would not have done them any good. They did not have the power to fight against antisemitism.

At the end of the year we got our report cards. Then our parents used to come to greet us. That year we noticed the non-Jewish boys were organizing; the other boys had prepared stones, bats, and metal balls on strings. We decided to run out early so they would stay and we would run home. We didn't stay for our report cards. The teachers' attitude was that we could not fight back. Jews were not supposed to fight back.

This is what we went through in Polish schools.

Thus passed my schooldays until 1939 when the Russians occupied Belitze.

Chapter Three
Soviet Occupation

At the beginning of World War II, the Russians were the allies of the Germans through the Nazi-Soviet Pact, a non-aggression treaty between the German Third Reich and the Soviet Union.[5] The pact was signed in Moscow on August 23, 1939, by the Soviet foreign minister Vyacheslav Molotov and the German foreign minister Joachim von Ribbentrop. The pact also agreed to a division of Poland between the two. From the east, the Russians occupied up to the Bug River, the boundary.

Jews had much more freedom when the Russians came. They were like our brothers. Everything was almost like heaven. We Jews had what we had always wanted—freedom. Nobody was criticizing us or hurting us. It was like a new world! We thought we would have the good life, that is, until we heard that Stalin had signed with Hitler. After this, we couldn't criticize Germany or Hitler or we would be punished.

The Russians looked after the children. They not only had the children listen to many speeches about Communism, but they also showed movies outdoors for the children as well as the adults. They came with huge buses with military singers and picked up the children, taking us for rides around the city and asking us to sing Russian songs. They gave us candy. Military dancers would also come to entertain us.

My brother, Mojshe, who was close with the police, was given a job by the Soviets to assess the harvests in Belitze and the vicinity. Each farmer would then know what percentage of the harvest was owed to the Soviet government. The farmers loved Mojshe because his assessments were always fair. Everybody said to my father, "Your son is gold." Mojshe didn't step on them or choke them. This was an important job to give to Mojshe who was only eighteen.

As part of our responsibilities to the government, we children were asked to help. We were proud to do that. We worked at the airport; the Soviets told us to clean up the area so that they could lay the asphalt for the runway. They were building an aerodrome (a hangar for airplanes). One day when we were

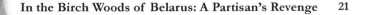

carrying supplies from one area to the other, we heard planes and bombing. Then we heard an explosion and saw huge flames. We asked the commander what was happening. He said, "Don't worry. The troops are on maneuvers; they are practicing. That's machine gun fire from the planes." But then a little later he told us that the war had started. He sent us all home in small groups through the woods; this way we would not be targets for the planes. We could see pieces of burnt paper flying. They were bombing Lida, thirty kilometers away. Lida was an important city, connecting with Vilna, Novogrodek, and Minsk; Lida was at this time an industrial center with factories and a railway-shipping center. Belitze had a strategic position with three roads running through the town to Lida, Žetel, Žaludek. There was also the bridge on the road to Žetel over the Neman River.

After this, we found out that on June 22, 1941, the Germans had turned on the Russians, despite the Hitler-Stalin Pact, and were attacking the Soviet Union. The Russians were retreating, moving east (see notes 1 and 4).

My brother Mojshe with a group of young men had decided to go east to escape the Germans. With tears in her eyes and a heavy heart, my mother packed Mojshe a new pair of shoes, food, and some money to take with him. She gave him new shoes so he could sell them for a piece of bread—if he had to.[6] Mother didn't know if she would ever see him again.

Mojshe and I were very attached. I looked up to him; he was my hero. He took me along everywhere he went; as children, we spent lots of fun times together. We slept together in the same bed.

I remember sometimes on weekends we used to go to the River Neman. Besides swimming and fishing we used to sneak into one of the docked boats that didn't belong to us. We were very scared, afraid we would be caught. We paddled a distance up the river. When we were upstream we would decorate the boat with branches and returning we lay back, drifting downstream with the current. These memories will stay with me forever. I loved him deeply with all my heart.

When Mojshe and his friends were on their way east, they passed our house. Mojshe ran into the house and asked my father to let me come with them. My father said, "No, he'll never make it. He's too skinny." Mojshe replied, "Dad, I'll carry him in my arms." Father wouldn't let him take me. My Aunt Hinda, the sister of my father, who was visiting us at the time, agreed with my father. Mojshe fell on the bed, grabbed his pillow, and cried and cried. Then he jumped up like a

crazy man and left to meet up with the group. I was sad to see him leave.

The farmers, too, were sad that Mojshe had gone away to the east. They said he was fair and treated them well.

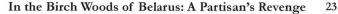

Chapter Four

The Germans

On Saturday, June 28, 1941, some boys and I were across from our house, in the schoolyard where there were apple trees. We had picked some apples off the ground and were lying around eating apples and relaxing. The day was very beautiful; I remember the sunlight on the trees. One of the boys was a Polish Jew from the Polish-German border. He saw a motorcycle with a soldier in a German uniform pass by—a scout for the Germans. This boy became wild, yelling, "The Germans are here." He jumped up like a lunatic, flew over the fence, and ran away like lightning. He had had plenty of experience with the Germans and was afraid of them. The rest of us ran home.

In no time the German soldiers came. In the evening many Polish greeted them, offering them bread and salt, the traditional symbols of welcome. We saw all this. But our father had not arrived home. We were worried because there was shooting on the streets—whoever they thought was Jewish or Russian was shot; the people may not have been Jewish or Russian but the Germans didn't care. They shot them if they thought they were. My mother was crying; she was wandering around half-crazed.

The Germans began to burn the houses—one big, huge flame over my town. The houses were made of wood and thatched with straw roofs; they burned quickly. Then the Germans were outside our house. They wouldn't let us leave the house. We thought we would burn to death. My Aunt Hinda came running and said, "Let them out. They are children—two boys and two girls—and their mother. One German agreed, yelling "*Raus. Raus.*" (Out, Out.) We ran over the fence and through gardens to the River Neman.

All the Jewish families met at this river. My mother was running around asking people if they had seen my father. No one had seen him, so they were concerned. All the Jews in town were like one family.

Early in the morning my father showed up with his clothes soaked in blood. A bullet had gone through his sleeve and grazed his arm. My mother cried when she saw him, especially when she saw the blood. My father said, "I'm okay. This

is nothing." She then told him that we first needed to find a place in which to live: the house was gone; the restaurant was gone. She asked him, "Is grandfather's house left?"

We went to my mother's father's little house and found that it had not been set on fire. My grandfather's house had not burned. *In fact, in 2000, the house was still there when we visited Belitze.* We moved into my grandfather's house and stayed there.

Later we moved into another house that had not burned—a larger, more comfortable house.

Chapter Five
My Father's Story

My father told us the following story about what had happened to him:

The Germans ordered twelve Jewish men brought to them. I was the twelfth. Then they lined us up. They gave us three minutes to live. They said, "If you can pray, pray." Then they machine-gunned us. We fell to the ground; I went down too. Maybe someone dragged me down. They shot us with another round. One, barely alive, started to scream in pain, screaming, "Please kill me."

A bullet from the first round went through the sleeve of my jacket but didn't even hit my arm. I fell to the ground like the rest and pretended I was dead. Then there was another round of fire. Luckily the wall of the house we had been stood against had caught fire. Just then it collapsed in flames and the Germans ran off to escape the heat and flames. I didn't know where you were, so I went to the Neman River where I had seen other Jews.

On the way back to the town he pointed out to us where he had stood. My father sadly remarked, "Here lie my friends. Of the twelve of us, only I remain." We saw the charred bodies. We recognized nothing but the coins we saw on their bodies. They had had change in their pockets. Only the coins they carried had not burnt. Their bodies were like charcoal; the money on top bright.

I saw this when I was fifteen years old!

Chapter Six

Mojshe

After the Germans arrived in Belitze, we had a number of other serious problems.

After he left Belitze, Mojshe had been caught by the Germans—by an advance guard of paratroopers. They had captured him and others. He decided to tell the Germans that he had been in jail and had managed to escape the Russians. He said to the Germans, "I'm free again. The Germans are our liberators." They gathered him and some others into a prisoner of war (POW) camp. They would take a few outside to check on them and Mojshe could hear machine gun fire. Then they would take another group and the same thing—the machine gun fire. They took Mojshe outside with one group but they didn't shoot him; Mojshe had light brown hair and he was circumcised but the Germans were doubtful; they weren't sure he was a Jew. Mojshe didn't "look Jewish"; he spoke Russian perfectly. They were going to take him outside again, but one Gentile stood up and said, "Why bother him. Don't you see? He's not a Jew; he's one of us." They released Mojshe later. He returned then to Belitze.

We were afraid they would pick him up again and kill him. At this time Mojshe was working, repairing motorcycles. He had learned at school in Żaludek, a nearby city, to be a mechanic; he stayed there with my father's sister, Aunt Belka. When Mojshe returned, he went to Mr. Dashkevitch, a Polish mechanic, who was very close with the Germans because he fixed their motorcycles. Mojshe asked Dashketich for a job. Mr. Dashkevitch was glad to hire Mojshe because he had been well trained.

His boss, Dashkevitch, and my brother Mojshe became friends; they were very close. He made sure that Mojshe did not wear the yellow star. He said to Mojshe, "I don't want you to feel scared." He tried to protect Mojshe. When the Germans came into the shop, they didn't know Mojshe was a Jew.

In town another Pole—Katanevitch—didn't like my brother. The two had a history going back before the war.

One winter day, before the war, my brother was in a tavern where they had beer, tea, and food. Katanevitch was there that evening and asked the Jewish girl for a warm beer; he ordered her to put

the beer into the oven to warm it. The girl said, "No, because the bottle will crack." He insisted and said that he would take the responsibility. The bottle cracked. The girl wanted him to pay.

My brother, who liked there to be harmony and peace, suggested that Katanevitch pay half and the girl pay half. Then Katanevitch interrupted my brother and said nasty things, such as "One dirty Jew standing up for another dirty Jew." My brother stood up (He was two years older than I but built differently—a strong man) and Katanevitch grabbed him by the shirt collar; then my brother grabbed him. Everybody at the tables got up and started saying, "A Jew is beating one of our brothers." My brother grabbed the stool he had been sitting on and went to the door, opened it, and said, "Everyone out of here."

A Jew, living next door to the tavern, saw what was going on and came running to my father, yelling, "Look what Mojshe is doing. They are going to make a pogrom." My father ran over with me behind him. I always followed my father. He went to the tavern, but the police had already come and taken Katanevitch to the police station. My brother had followed the Russian police, to whom Katanevitch was complaining about the Jews: "G-d damn, dirty Jews." Each time he said something my brother kicked him in his butt. When they got into the police station, the secretary, a Polish man, who heard and saw all this, said, "I quit." My brother grabbed him and told him, "Sit back down there and don't move. You're not going anywhere." My brother had a good relationship with the police; they knew he was not a troublemaker.

Therefore, when the Germans came, Katanevitch said, "Before it was your government. Now it's mine. I'm going to teach you a lesson." When he heard this, my brother went to his boss and told him what Katanevitch had said. The boss sent for Katanevitch and gave him orders, "When you see Mojshe on the street, you don't know him. If you bother him, I'll take care of you." The boss knew he could protect my brother because Dashkevitch was friends with the mayor, Balabonski, who didn't like Jews, even though my father had helped him when the mayor had been in financial trouble, giving him a place to sleep in one of the rooms of the restaurant, food, and one shot glass of whiskey a day (he wouldn't give him more). Balabonski liked his drink. All of this was free of charge. My father said to him, "The room rent is free, and I'll give you food and a shot a day."

The mayor who was close to the Germans never betrayed my brother and neither did Katanevitch. The Germans used to pick up Jews for labor battalions. One day they picked up my brother Richard, but Balabonski sent him home and kept the other Jewish boys. Richard thanked Balabonski. Balabonski said, "You're lucky your father's name is Shmulka."

Chapter Seven

The Germans "Play"

Another problem we had with the Germans occurred when they wanted to "play with us," as a cat plays with a mouse; however, the Germans ridiculed, tortured, and killed. Whenever they came into our town, they had to kill people.

One day they rounded up Rabbi Shabtai Fein and some other Jews. A local policeman, Garniak, saw my father on the street and told him, "Go home and hide." He saved our lives. We went to my grandfather's house to the garden and hid among the growing vegetables. We could hear but could not see what was happening.

The Christians who watched later told us exactly what had happened. They told the thirty-six Jews to wash the horses. Outside the Russian Orthodox Church they tortured the rabbi. I still can hear the rabbi groaning; his voice, crying: "Oy! Oy! Oy!" We were told by them that the rabbi's beard was shaved off with a hand saw and that they had had the rabbi wash the horses' hooves and then forced him to drink the dirty water. Then they tied him to a horse and dragged him. They had prepared graves for the thirty-six. The Nazis shot these Jews and threw them into the graves—some still alive. I saw this grave; after a week or so, the grave had sunk lower and lower. You could see cracks in the earth. I saw a hand sticking out.

The Germans continued to pick up people for *Juden Spiel* (Jew Games). Once I was rounded up with my father. My cousin Hirshe Leizer, the Hebrew teacher, the one who loved the Polish teacher, Civia, was with us. He was shaking. My father said to both of us, "Nothing is going to happen."

The Germans wanted "to play" with us. They lined us up in front of the church in a large open area. Next door was the Polish school, which was surrounded by a wooden picket fence. The Germans pulled off the slats from the fence; some slats still had nails in them. The Germans surrounded us, lying on the ground with machine guns pointed at us, so we wouldn't try to run off. The ones with the slats lined up, making a gauntlet for us to run through. My father comforted me. He said, "Everything will be okay. Don't give up." At the beginning of the gauntlet a German officer with a hard rubber whip clobbered us in the face and on our backs. Then they forced us to run the gauntlet of soldiers who beat us

with the slats, even with the ones that had nails in them. Someone put his foot out to trip me so that I would fall and they could beat me to death. I tripped, ran out of the line by accident, and I kept running. They called, "Halt!" and I halted. They brought me back and I had to begin again with the whip in the face and back. I was fifteen years old and had to go through this. We went home afterwards. I was beyond feeling pain. Although my body was bruised, I was numb. Mother cried and bathed our cuts with cold water.

Now I knew what to expect when I saw the German uniform.

Persons who toured Belarussia at the close of the war reported that it had been turned into a wasteland. It is estimated that over 200 towns and 9,200 villages were destroyed during the three years of Nazi occupation. Official postwar estimates of human losses suggest that 2.3 million citizens, or one out of every four people in Belarussia, perished during the war and Nazi occupation. The most conservative estimate of the civilian casualties during the war is 1.4 million. This is in addition to the 250,000 Belorussian Jews who are estimated to have perished. (Wytwycky, Bohdan. *The Other Holocaust: Many Circles of Hell.* Novak Report: 1980. 70.)

Chapter Eight

Surviving the Germans

When the Germans occupied Belitze, we had to watch every move the Germans made. The police, local young men, would tell us that the Germans needed twenty or so people for labor. When we showed up for this unpaid labor, they had whips and hit us numerous times. The local police were almost as brutal as the Germans.

The Germans continued to harass us. They would round us up for labor detachments, for example, to clear snow off the highways with shovels. Every day one or two were arbitrarily killed. If the Germans wanted to go to another village, instead of using horses, they would round up people. They chose Jewish shop owners to pull wagons five or six miles to another village.

We learned to hide when we saw the police and Germans preparing to round us up for work. Our parents would send us to hide in the fields. We would lie in the fields all day. If the field was planted with corn, it was easy to hide there among the stalks. But these were potato fields. We had to lie down flat so no one would see us. After the Germans had gone, our parents would come and tell us to come home.

Sometimes my father, Richard, and I hid in other places. Usually chopped pieces of wood were stacked against the wall of the stable. To make a hiding place, father stacked the wood a little away from the stable wall. When the Germans came into town we hid there. Sometimes father hid outside and sometimes inside the house. We didn't feel good about leaving mother in the house. However, the Germans at this time rarely bothered women, so mother stayed inside with the girls, Katie and Ida.

Life went on like this until they took us to the ghetto.

Chapter Nine

The Ghetto

At the beginning of November 1941, the mayor ordered us to wear the yellow star, front and back, and to leave Belitze and go to a designated ghetto—all this by February 22, 1942. They made sure all were in a ghetto, either in Lida or Žetel (Yiddish: Žetel; Russian: Zhatlava) (pronounce: Djatlava Zhetel). Our family went to Žetel Ghetto. We could not go even one foot outside the boundaries. To ensure this, the Germans built a wooden wall with barbed wire on the top. We lived with two or three families in one house, and all shared their food, their flour and potatoes.

Two local policemen guarded the gate. The Jews were not even permitted to talk to other citizens and might be shot if they attempted to obtain food from the outside. Nevertheless, peasants still brought food to the ghetto to exchange it for gold, clothes, and other items. Special work permits were issued to those who worked outside the ghetto. The Jews were guarded when marched in columns out of the ghetto to perform forced labor. (ushmm.org)

The leader of the *Judenrat* (Jewish council) for the Žetel Ghetto, Dvoretski, a lawyer and a very educated man, had to satisfy the Nazi demands.[7] Whenever the Nazis came into the ghetto, he presented them with a cake with a golden ring on top; however he always had a pistol in his pocket for his own protection. Each time they met, the Germans demanded more and more from the Jewish community: money, gold, furs, ...

Once they demanded fifty pairs of leather boots and said they would kill the same number of Jews if we didn't produce the boots. The shoemakers did have leather; they thought the war would be over soon and they could go back to business with the leather they had saved. They worked day and night to finish the fifty pairs of boots that the Germans wanted.

Eventually our ghetto had exhausted all its resources: money, gold, furs, and leather, although we had gone house to house to collect. We sometimes got resources from another ghetto. However, it reached a point where the German demands could no longer be fulfilled.

The Germans would kill Jews for minor incidents, such as for smuggling in bread from the outside. For smuggling incidents such as this they would shoot the whole family as an example to the rest of the ghetto to discourage smuggling.

Finally in April 1942, the Germans wanted the area *Judenrein*, cleansed of Jews. This is when Dvoretski, the leader of *Judenrat*, decided that a resistance group should be organized. They bought guns from farmers who had gotten the guns from the Russians when they were retreating; maybe they had dropped them. The Germans caught Shalom Fiolon (a Jewish man), who had a gun, so they tortured him. He would not give any information. They beat him so badly that his lungs were damaged. He was spitting blood. (See note 7.)

Dvoretski was very concerned about what was happening to the imprisoned Shalom. He somehow always found an excuse to send someone from the ghetto to do some work around the jail. On the ground under the window where Shalom was locked up, they found little pieces of crumbled up notes soaked in blood from the beatings. The notes repeated the same message, always the same: "I'm being tortured, but don't worry; I won't tell."

Finally he was murdered. No more notes were found.

We learned that the Germans planned to liquidate the ghetto on April 28, 1942. Dvoretski escaped and went to the woods with quite a few, maybe thirty or forty men, to join a partisan group.[8] Because he was the leader of the *Judenrat*, he had access to money, guns, and ammunition. He had plans to get more people out of the ghetto, but he wasn't lucky.

While in the woods with the rest of the men, Dvoretski met the group leader of the Russian partisans—a man by the name of Kola Verchonin. After a few days Verchonin realized that Dvoretski was very capable and felt threatened by him. Therefore, he shot Dvoretski in his sleep, murdering him. He feared that eventually Dvoretski would take over the leadership. Moreover, Verchonin took his gun and boots.[9] Thus, Verchonin remained the leader of the whole partisan group.

It happened on many occasions that a Russian partisan shot a Jewish partisan just for his gun, leather jacket, or boots.

The principle reason for the multiplication of the partisan bands—besides the terror and oppression of Nazi rule—was the favorable terrain, broken by many forests and marshes. Guerrilla formations, both Soviet controlled and independent, were estimated to include as many

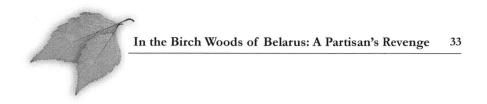

as 300,000 fighters. The guerrillas were able to disrupt Nazi control often and successfully. The Nazis retaliated with demonstrations of brutality upon the nearest citizens, however innocent.

(Wytwycky, Bohdan. *The Other Holocaust: Many Circles of Hell*. Novak Report: 1980. 67.)

Chapter Ten

Escape from the Ghetto

My brother Mojshe belonged to a group of about twenty or twenty-two men. When Mojshe heard about the liquidation, he went to the woods with this group of men to meet up with the partisans.

After a short time as a partisan Mojshe was killed by the Germans and the police. The Germans had surrounded a clearing. As the partisan group went through this clearing that they had thought was safe, the Germans opened fire from all four sides. The partisans didn't have a chance. One partisan, Jankel Orzhechowski, survived by jumping into the bushes where he wasn't noticed.

After our family escaped the ghetto, we met Jankel. Jankel told us that my brother had escaped; Jankel said he had seen Mojshe running, running. My father and I didn't believe Jankel, but he insisted this was the truth. Out of pain and concern and to make Jankel tell us the truth, as if to stab himself, my father grabbed a knife, which I immediately took away from him. Jankel continued lying. He lied to protect my parents from pain.

A few days later—this was after Mojshe had left—my family escaped the ghetto because we were warned that, on April 28, 1942, all the Jews in the Žetel Ghetto were to be taken outside the ghetto, massacred, and buried. We went into a hiding place under a small stable—8' x 12.' My brother, Richard, sisters Katie and Ida, my parents, and three more people—neighbors—hid there. We made a shallow, square box and filled this with manure. Under this we had made a hole. We would get in the hole and pull the box over the hole to cover our hiding place. The Germans would open the door and look around, but they didn't see anything but manure. We stayed there until night on the day the ghetto was liquidated. We heard a lot of explosions.

My father looked through the hole of the pipe we used for air and said, "They just got your mother's sister Bashe Malke, her husband Shimen, and the baby (two or three months old)." They had hidden in another place under the floor of a house. My father continued, "They took them outside; she is holding the baby. Oh G-d, a German is choking the baby to death in his mother's arms.

Now he is killing Bashe! And her husband is watching. The German beast killed Bashe's husband." Can you imagine the brutality of this!

Then we found out that my cousin, Hirshe Leizer, the Hebrew teacher, who had been with us and was married to Civia, and now with a little baby, was hiding too. The baby started to cry. The others said, "Smother the baby or they'll find us." Hirshe said, 'I am not killing my baby. I'll go out." He went out, and they killed him; they threw in hand grenades and everybody was murdered, including Civia and the baby.

We learned later that the Jews of Belitze had been herded into the Kino (the movie theatre) from which the SS packed them into trucks, taking them near the old cemetery to huge pits in the Kurpishtz Forest where thousands were massacred.

We also heard that on August 6, 1942, the remaining Jews of Żetel were ordered to gather at the marketplace and its close-by buildings and 2500 of them were killed at the new cemetery. After these two massacres, the Jewish community of Żetel came to an end after having existed for 450 years. (zhetel.org)

This horror was our life every day. I never dreamed we would ever get out. This goes for the ghetto, the partisans, and whatever else I went through.

Night came. Father said, "I am going to walk out first. If you hear shooting, don't come out." He left. There were no shots. We did not wait. Without hesitation, my mother, then the children, and then the neighbors followed my father and so we left the hiding place. It was dark but flames flared occasionally. My father took a stick and held it over his shoulder so if anybody saw this they would think he had a rifle.

We made it to the woods and slept there. We saw no partisans. We had no food, except wild berries. At night my mother went to the village from house to house asking for a slice of bread. She would not let us go because it was too dangerous. I saw my mother leaving and I didn't know if she would ever come back. Life was treacherous.

We were looking for a safe place to settle. We saw a place close to houses. But could the occupants be trusted? Would they betray us? This place was not far from a house occupied by a family named Shavel. We felt safe even though we were not close to him. He could give us news about the Germans. He couldn't give us much food, however, because he was poor.

Finally the Germans decided to go into the woods and kill the "Stalin dogs," what the Germans called the partisans. Everybody heard the news and abandoned their hiding places. We ran deeper into the forest. We had to run through creeks. My boots got wet. It had been rainy and the ground was deep with mud; then it turned cold and the ground froze. My feet were frostbitten. They swelled so much that they had to cut my boots off.

The Germans were still searching in the woods; we were short of places to hide. To be safe we dug an underground shelter that we shored up with saplings so it wouldn't cave in. There were steps going up to the door. Inside there were bunks. We made torches from moss and sticks, lighting these with a flint stone. Sometimes we would inhale soot, the residue of these torches. Eight or nine people, including my family, lived in this bunker—Majewski, his wife, and a baby, Sanford. The baby caused us anxiety because if the baby cried our bunker could have been discovered. The father said, "If you want my baby killed, *you* kill him." So one of them put pillows over the baby's face. When they lifted the pillows, the baby was still breathing. They saw that this baby was meant to live. After this, they all agreed not to kill the baby, no matter what happened. The parents wanted to give their baby to a non-Jew; however, this man saw that the mother was having a hard time giving the baby away, so he said no. *That baby, Sanford, is alive today with a family of his own. We were invited to his wedding.*

When the Germans were in the woods looking for Jews, all the others from the bunker, except me, would leave the bunker and go deeper into the woods to hide. I could not leave; because of my frostbitten feet, I could not walk. When they left they would cover the opening of the shelter with wood to which they had attached moss and pieces of branches to camouflage the opening. I would be in the bunker hiding. I would hear the Germans calling to each other. I often would hear horses trotting and whinnying. Once a horse stepped right next to me. If his hoof had been any closer, he and his rider would have been in the hole with me and I would have been killed. I had to wait in the bunker until the rest returned.

When the Germans were not searching for Jews and we were all in the bunker, I would sometimes climb out and put my feet in the sun. That seemed to help cure the sores and cracks in my feet. During the night my feet would crack again. The next day I would start over again with my feet in the sun. I could feel the skin forming during the day and then at night it would crack again. I would wrap

my feet in burlap potato bags—these were dirty—full of mud and sand, but they were all I had. It was a wonder my feet did not become infected. In my old age, my feet are numb from the frostbite and I have trouble walking.

I tried to keep clean, using the snow to wash and rinse myself. We had to wear the same clothes all the time. In the spring when it was warmer, I would bathe and wash my clothes in a creek.

We had to move deeper into the woods to hide from the Germans who continued searching for Jews. I had to walk, leaning on two sticks, like crutches. I was in pain and very thirsty. One day I was so thirsty that when I saw a spot where a horse had urinated and the snow had melted, I knelt down and sucked the melted snow.

With me I had a hand grenade without the lever and a gun without ammunition. They were of no use to me but I kept them, hoping, I guess, that I would run into ammunition for the gun and a lever to arm the grenade. Eventually my feet were somewhat better. We continued hiding in the woods. We would still go to the villagers to ask for some food. We would go out and get potatoes and bread and bring these back. Sometimes the partisans would drop off some food.

That was our life for a while until one day a group of partisans came along to see us and give us information, dropping off some potatoes. They had heard that someone had buried a gun in the vicinity, so they had come and dug up the gun. It had been buried in the woods, wrapped in oiled cloth. While they were visiting with us, they asked me if I wanted to be a partisan. I said, "Yes, but I don't have a good gun nor any ammunition." To be allowed to join the partisans a person would usually need to bring a gun and ammunition or they didn't want him. But they said they had an extra rifle. They gave me the rifle—the buried one.

The partisans also received weapons from Russian planes that dropped ammunition and dynamite attached to parachutes. At the same time, they would also drop a Russian officer who made sure the partisans received the ammunition. For the time being, he became part of the partisans group.

The partisans would then make signal fires for the planes—in different designs at different times—so that they not only would know where to drop the supplies but also so that the Germans would not anticipate where they would be dropping the supplies. On rare occasions the planes circled but did not drop any supplies, as if they had intelligence that the drop was unsafe. This was disturbing

to us, waiting for supplies that were desperately needed.

The partisans told me to ask my father if I could join them. I walked up to my father and said, "I would like to become a partisan. They have a rifle for me." He said, "My son, do what you think is right and G-d should watch over you." Thus, I joined the partisans (see note 8).

Chapter Eleven

The Bridge

I found out that my first mission as a partisan was to help them destroy the long wooden bridge over the Neman River, near the village of Mishilovce (see Photographs section). Many German trucks transversed this bridge. We had to destroy the bridge because it was an important connection to other cities; destroying it would disrupt enemy communications.

We were about thirteen partisans on this mission. When we arrived at the huge woods near the bridge, they pulled in among the trees with the horses and wagon. They told me about the mission and then gave me the following order, "Stay here. If you see the Germans turn into the village of Mishilovce, shoot this rifle to warn us because if the Germans pull into the village, we will be in danger." I was scared to death. I held the rifle close to my chest. This rifle was the one they had dug up in the woods and although it had been wrapped in oiled cloth, it had not been well cleaned. If I had shot it, it may have backfired and I could have been killed. *I didn't know this at the time; I found this out later.* They said, "When we are finished, we'll fire a pistol to signal everybody back to the horses and then we'll leave together.

I stayed in the woods watching and waiting. It was so quiet that I could hear the leaves falling off the trees. I could hear the horses snorting. I stood there holding the rifle close to my body, so the rifle would not be seen.

This bridge was a fairly new bridge, ½ kilometer long, built by the Polish army just before the war (see Photographs section). As I waited, I saw the small black out lights on the German trucks. (These lights were for use during black out periods so that the planes wouldn't bomb them.) The partisans went on to the bridge and began to nail down rubber strips every few feet. Whenever a German truck drove over, the partisans, who were nailing down the rubber strips, hid under the bridge in the bridge trusses. When they had finished, they poured gasoline on the strips and then lit the gasoline-soaked strips, setting them on fire. When the villagers of Mishilowcze saw the flames, they ran out to put out the fire. To scare them, the partisans shot machine gun fire over their heads—a

roof of fire—and the villagers ran back to their village. After this, the partisans returned to where I was waiting. We got into our wagons and took off back to base camp.

On the way back we were spotted by German planes near a power mill run by water. We were riding on a trail for horses and wagons. The planes that spotted us knew it was partisan territory, so they opened fire. We scrambled off the wagons and ran into a field nearby the mill. They hit the building but not us. Then we got back into the wagons and finally came to base. At almost sixteen years old, I became one of these men.

The bridge was completely destroyed, burned to ashes. In the newspaper, the Germans reported that they had killed 500 partisans, taken a number of prisoners, and had recovered much ammunition. Propaganda for the villagers to discourage them from joining the partisans!

Chapter Twelve
The Spy

Another time while I was in the partisans I was on night duty at an outpost, approximately a kilometer away from base. A nasty night—cold, windy, rainy— and I didn't feel good. I had a terrible toothache; my face was swollen; my cheeks puffed out. The pain was so severe that it brought me to my knees, crouched, holding my rifle. I supported myself with the rifle. Then I closed my eyes trying to think. In my mind, I envisioned my brother Mojshe coming toward me in old clothes. While this was happening, the person who watches to see if the guards stay awake came along. If he takes a person's rifle to headquarters, that person is dead. They would shoot him for dereliction of duty.

He came and tried to take my rifle. He said, "You were asleep." I said, "No. I am like this because I have a toothache and the weather is so bad." Finally I was taken to a building where they housed sick partisans. While I was there, there was a knock on the door. Some partisans from our base had caught a spy. These partisans were on a mission, so they asked me to take the spy to our base camp. The others were too sick to walk. Therefore, there was no one else but me to walk to base with the spy.

This base camp was guarded on the parameters and in the middle was a huge fire where people were sitting. When it is so bitter cold, the fire feels good! That night the spy, too, sat and waited but *he* complained about the heat. I made him stay in front. He told us that he had been looking for his wife, his pregnant wife. He said that she must have gotten lost. We knew about her. She had been questioned and it was determined that she was a spy. She was then taken out and executed.

Early in the morning a group came back from a mission. The leader, Arke Gertzowski, was a great man. I worshipped him as a hero. This man, a strong man, from Novogrodek, had been the neighbor of the spy. Arke recognized him. He acted as if he were happy—his face lit up as if with joy. Arke walked up to the spy, calling him by his first name, and then said, "My friend, I never thought I'd see you here. My wife and children—I hated them. I'm so glad that you brought

the Germans to my home and that they killed my wife and children." Shocked, I was staring at him, as were the other men in the group. Arke began to roll a cigarette and then offered the spy some tobacco to roll into a cigarette. As the spy was rolling the tobacco, Arke slapped him hard in the face and the spy fell down. Arke was not a tall man but built like a bull. Arke fell on the spy and began beating him. We had to grab Arke and keep them apart. This could not be allowed to continue because the spy had to be questioned. By this time it was dawn and they took him into the headquarters building. After questioning him, they sent him, walking, on a trail through the forest, with a partisan following him on horseback. We heard several shots. He, too, had been executed.

Chapter Thirteen
The Truth about Mojshe

Clouds pour across the moon. Anger leaves a poisonous dark-green bruise on the sky

—"Clouded sky," Miklós Radnóti

Once I was on a dangerous mission with Jankel, the one who had been with Mojshe in the clearing. That night (our missions were always at night; we hid during the day) while we were on our way to the village, I asked Jankel again for the truth about my brother Mojshe: "I would like to know what happened to Mojshe. I know you know. You were there." He replied, "Mojshe ran and ran until he reached another section of the woods. He is in the other woods." The partisan groups had different names. Our woods were the *Lipichanska Puscha* (see note 8). I said, "Jankel, we have no guarantee that we are going to survive this mission. Before I die, I want you to tell me about my brother." He still tried to back out. It took me time to convince him: I told him, "This is a dangerous mission, and we both may be killed. Before we die, I would like to know what happened to Mojshe. I'll never forgive you if you don't tell me." Jankel eventually relented, saying, "Give me your hand. Promise me you will not tell your parents." I promised. He gave me his hand and we shook hands as a pledge.

Jankel told me this story: He had told us before that he had last seen Mojshe running out of the clearing and had seen him continue to run away from the Germans and the Polish police. Now Jankel admitted that my brother had been wounded, so the police pulled off his boots, took his ammunition and clothes, and then took him away. Jankel saw this from the bushes where he was hiding.

Our partisan group knew what happened to a partisan who was shot and captured by the Germans. He would be taken to a hospital where his wounds would be healed. Doesn't this sound humane? However, when the partisan was healed, the Germans would force the near by villagers to come to see a "show." To avoid this, if the partisan group knows where the prisoner is taken, the group will attack the hospital, kill the Germans, and try to save their fellow partisan.

This "show" was a warning to anyone who might be thinking about becoming a partisan about the consequences if caught. The captured partisan, naked, is put on a platform, held by two SS on either side, and a proclamation is read. The audience is told, "This is what we do with Stalin's dogs." The partisan's hands are shut in a door and thus broken until just the skin is hanging down. Then his arms are stretched back until the joints pop apart. Now the prisoner is helpless. Bayonets begin to slice pieces of flesh from his body and these pieces of flesh are thrown off the stage, so people will see and be warned. This continues until the partisan bleeds to death.

So when I heard from Jankel that Mojshe had been captured, I was sick to my stomach. I knew what they would have done to him. I wanted to die. I vowed to avenge him.[10] I was not afraid of the Germans anymore. I asked G-d to take me to my brother.

Chapter Fourteen

The Raid

Jankel and I continued on our night mission. I was sick at heart because of what I had heard about Mojshe.

We had been ordered to go to this village to bring out nine policemen, Polish and White Russians, who were collaborating with the Germans. We were supposed to bring them out alive so we could get information from them. If we could not bring them out alive, we were supposed to bring them out dead.

Before we went into the village, we had sent a rider to be sure all dogs were in the houses so that they wouldn't bark. If a dog were left outside, we would shoot it with a silencer on the rifle. The villagers were also supposed to turn out all their kerosene lamps.

We went into the village where those policemen resided. Two partisans were at each house, one in the front and one at the back or side door. This was to ensure that nobody left the house. The house I was responsible for had two doors, one in the front and one on the side. I was still with Jankel. We were supposed to get a signal—a pistol shot—to go into the house. We heard the signal and knocked on the window.

A woman came to the window and told us she was all by herself because the Germans had taken her husband, and her children were not home. She said, "I won't open the door." So we knocked out the window frame and climbed in. We searched all over—under the bed and behind doors, all over. There was no one. We didn't find any police. Maybe they were on duty. We did find huge boxes—chests for clothes. I looked into the boxes and found Jewish goods: silver candleholders and tablecloths for *Shabbos* (Sabbath dinner)—robbed from Jewish homes. There were also sheets, coats, and suits. We took the goods and put some on our wagon. There was not enough room on the one wagon for all these precious treasures, so we asked the woman for her horse and wagon. She fought with us. I was still angry about my brother's death, so I pushed her aside and left her on the floor. We took the horse and wagon, loading up all the goods and took them back to base.

Again the same propaganda exaggerating out losses and glorifying the German

gains. Next day the Germans reported that there had been a great battle and that they had killed hundreds of partisans and captured a great deal of ammunition.

We returned to base.

After this, I remember, a time that we were surrounded by Germans looking for "Stalin's dogs." We had no food for days. I came upon a dead horse covered in maggots. (I had smelled it first.) I scraped the maggots off and saw that the meat was mushy. But I had no choice; I had to eat something.

I took the steel wire from my rifle and scraped the meat. Then I made a fire and blackened it so that I could eat it without vomiting.

Chapter Fifteen

Istrabitilsky Battalion

I was in the partisans until the Soviets came back after they had defeated the Germans at the Battle of Stalingrad in Russia during the winter of 1942-1943.[11] The German army was now very weak. I came home to Belitze in 1943 when I was recruited by the *Istrabitilsky Battalion*, in some ways similar to the Soviet Secret Police.[12] The *Istrabitilsky Battalion* was established by the Soviet military to keep order in the occupied territory, including Belitze. Belarus was not completely liberated until July of 1944.

I was never scared. I didn't care if I died. I was eighteen years old; I wanted revenge for my brother Mojshe and for what the Germans had done to my father, mother, and siblings in our village and in the ghetto.

Our battalion had orders to clear the forest of the German soldiers who were retreating from the Soviet Union. The Germans were at this point losing the war and during the retreat they were taking what they needed, such as food and livestock, from the local farmers, who were suffering. We were ordered to dress in German uniforms so we could take them unaware. The Russians ordered us not to kill. They said, "If you kill a German, we'll bury you in the same grave."

I wondered to myself why the Russians were not killing the Germans because the German army had been brutal as the army made its way east to Stalingrad—burning homes and farms, raping and killing people. The Russian leaders said they wanted to capture as many Germans as they could without loss of Soviet lives. If the Germans heard that the Russians were treating German prisoners of war (POWs) well, then more German soldiers would surrender without further bloodshed.

One day the Russian officer told me to have the ten POWs, whom we had captured, move wet logs that were very heavy because the bark was water-soaked. He said, "Let two POWS carry one log." I said, "Let each of them carry one. Why should they have an easy time?" So the captured Germans moved the logs. Then the Russian officer told me to tell them to sit down and take a rest. While they were taking a break, the officer and I rolled cigarettes out of a piece of newspaper and loose tobacco. One of the Germans asked me to give him a cigarette. Because we

were instructed by the officer to treat them well, I wanted to show him that I was being fair. I gave everyone of them paper and tobacco to roll his own cigarette. As we were smoking and relaxing, a plane flew over. The Russian officer told me to ask the POWs, "How come you were once so strong but now our planes are flying and yours are not? And why are you prisoners now?" After I asked them, one with a shaved head stood up. He had probably been an officer; his posture was erect and he looked down on people. He was arrogant. He answered, "We'll still be in Moscow drinking champagne."

I remember clearly one mission for the battalion right before the Russians took me into the army. Moishe Rappaport, a Polish Jew, who had escaped the Germans (our community had welcomed him, taking him in), and I were ordered to interrogate a certain farmer. We were told that this farmer was giving the Germans leads about where to find supplies, such as cattle, chickens, and geese. We were supposed to make this farmer tell us when the Germans would be coming for information.

The farmer's name sounded familiar to me. Then I remembered that he knew my father. My father was well known in the area because he had the liquor store and restaurant. I told Moishe Rappaport this. I said to Moishe, "I'll go in first. I'll tell him my name and see if I can convince him to set up the Germans, so we can capture them." Moishe stayed outside on guard. I went in and introduced myself to this farmer. I said, "I am the son of Shmulka—even though I am in a German uniform. I came here to talk with you. I want to save you. We had had a report that you are telling the Germans where to find supplies. What we want you to do is to tell us when the Germans are coming here to talk with you, so we can ambush them." He said, "I don't know what you are talking about." I said, "You should help us. You'd better tell me because I came here to save your life. I want to save your life. If you don't tell me, the Russians will tie your hands and feet, lock you and your family in your home, and burn the house down with you in it. I don't want this to happen to you." He refused to help us. He said. "I don't know about anything." I went out and told Moishe, who then went in to try to convince the farmer to tell us about the Germans. He still refused. Moishe came out and we left. I never knew what happened to the farmer.

Chapter Sixteen
A German

On the way back to the base we saw a German walking, crossing a trail—one of the deserters from the Eastern Front in Russia. I knew if he saw us first he would shoot us. I told Moishe Rappaport to tell the German to drop his gun and ammunition. The German soldier lay down and then we lay down. Moishe hollered in German (he spoke German like a German, probably had come from some border town): "Stop. Throw away your rifle and raise your hands." I said, "Tell him to stand up. You cover me." I walked over to him and took his gun and checked him out to be sure he didn't have a concealed weapon. This German had a towel around his neck. There was dried blood on his uniform—not recent, but days or maybe even weeks old. When the Germans first marched into Poland, they were smiling, clean, and happy. Now they were unhappy and dirty; we could smell them from a distance.

We stopped at a house where a man had a horse and wagon so we told the man to take us in his wagon to Belitze. Outside Belitze we stopped and set the German down. Then we sent the man back home with his wagon. We took the German off the main road to a side road that went downhill, where no one could see us. We were about one kilometer from a mill. From the road we saw a grove of birch saplings.

As I looked at this German, I was remembering the destruction of Belitze. I was remembering my cousin Hirshe Leizer, Civia, and their baby—all murdered, and the murder of my other cousins and their baby. I was remembering Mojshe and the pieces of his flesh being thrown to the dogs. I felt a murderous rage. (See note 10.)

This German was young and arrogant. I told him to take off the towel. A bullet had gone through his neck. He had a leather bag with bread and a bottle of milk. I asked him, "Why are you carrying bread and milk? The soldier said, "I can't swallow too good. So I eat the bread and drink the milk at the same time." I told Moishe, "Let me handle this." I asked the German three questions:

"How many soldiers have you killed?" He said, "None."

I asked, "How many partisans have you killed?" He said, "None."

I asked him, "How many Jews have you killed?" He replied, "None."

I said, "Then what did you do in the army?" He answered, "I was a shoemaker."

I said, "Then what are you doing with a gun?" My brother was on my mind, in my heart, and in my bones. I then told the German to take off his shoes. He took them off.

Then he closed his eyes, so he wouldn't see us shooting him. A few seconds went by and he opened his eyes. I told him to raise his hands. He put his hands up. Then one hand came down and he put one hand on his heart, pleading for his life, "Comrades, spare my life. I have a wife and two little children at home." He then opened his eyes and put his hand between his jacket and his shirt. I yelled, "What are you doing?" He took out a photograph and showed it to us. It was a photo of a woman holding children by their hands. I said, "You have a beautiful wife and beautiful children. Take a good look at them. You'll never see them again." I shot him and he fell to the ground. I could tell he wasn't dead, so Moishe and I each put a bullet into him.

I had seen a little house nearby, so we went there. We wanted to wash our hands and get a bite to eat. The woman gave us water and a towel. She had already prepared *blini* (a flat, fried wheat bread). She gave us some with buttermilk. I told her that I had seen a dead German in the woods near her house. I said, "I'd like you to bury him." She said, "My dear boys! My dear boys! The Germans took my husband away. I cannot do that." I told her if she didn't want to be killed that she had to bury the body. I told her, "Listen. We'll come back later to check. If we come back and find him, we'll bury you with him." I never went to check to see if she had.

Chapter Seventeen
With my Parents

When I was in the *Istrabitilsky Battalion*, whatever I did I never told my parents. I didn't want them to know. However, other people talked. After the war not many Jews were left in my town. But elderly Jewish survivors got together as if they were one family and often talked when they met on the street. After one of our missions, Jankel Orzhechowski talked to this group that included my father. He told them about the eight Germans. The group asked him, "Who was with you?" Jankel mentioned my name. So in this way my father heard about the eight Germans and what Jankel and I had done to them.

On this particular mission we had captured eight German soldiers. I was with Jankel, the same Jankel who had told me what had happened to Mojshe. I guess because I was with Jankel, on the way back to the base camp memories of my tortured brother entered my mind. I thought of Mojshe and I thought again of the horrible way they had choked my aunt's three months-old baby. They had done this while the baby lay in his mother's arms, to torture his parents who were watching. I thought of the countless murderous acts the Germans had perpetrated on helpless and innocent people, especially on children.

In that state of mind I was overcome with rage, as was Jankel, so we decided to shoot the eight. (See note 10.)

That day when I came home, my father was waiting at the door. I had my rifle on my shoulder. He slapped me in my face. I saw stars flying. I was shocked; I hadn't expected this. My mother said, "Take off the rifle and sit down to dinner." So I put the rifle in a corner and sat at the table. My father always sat at the head.

He said, "Don't you want to know why I slapped you?" I said, "No, I guess you know that." He answered, "How could you stand up people who have the same nose, eyes, and mouth as you and kill them?" I replied, "How did you feel when they stood you up against the wall—twelve against that wall and machine-gunned you? How did you like it? All the rest are dead. You were all covered in blood from your friends." He said, "If they are murderers, do you have to be a murderer?" I did not want to tell him about the fate of his son—how Mojshe had died.

Thanks to Hitler and the Nazi regime, I, who, before the war, was this peaceful village boy, learning to be a barber, was turned into a "murderer." These events left permanent scars.

After I married and found out what my wife, who was only twelve years old, went through in the concentration camps, and after I heard about the things that happened to other people, I am very proud I did what I did. I am only sorry I did not do more. Saying this, however, does not mean that I do not have scars.

Chapter Eighteen

In the Russian Army

I received a notice, telling me to come immediately to the draft board at Lida, thirty kilometers from Belitze. The partisans had said, "After the Russians return, we will have a vacation." However, when the partisans came out of the woods, they were sent right to the front lines. No uniforms. No time. Because the Russians were pushing ahead and the Germans were on the run, they needed men in the Red Army. I knew two people from my town that went into the Red Army. These people never came back.

I went to Lida still wearing my German uniform; I didn't have any other clothes. I had sewn a red stripe on the uniform cap to show that I was not a German. I wanted to get a job working for the Soviet government; I was told that if I had a job, the Soviets wouldn't draft me. I went there and talked to the person in charge. We were chatting, and he asked me where I was during the war. I told him that I was in the *Arlanski Atrad*. He said, "I was a partisan too." He gave me a document to take to the Russians to show them I had a job. I felt secure then.

In ten days I got another card: "Come to the draft board immediately." I didn't know what to do, but I knew I had an exemption, a document that said I couldn't be drafted. I went back to that partisan; he reassured me: "Don't worry about it. Take the exemption certificate to the army and show it to them."

So I went to the draft board. There was one guy ahead of me. When it was my turn, I told the man in charge, "I have a document that I have a job so I am exempt" He said, "Let me see that." He didn't even look at it. He tore the document into pieces and threw it away, banging his hand on the desk. "A healthy, strong guy like you not going to fight. Who do you think will protect Mother Russia for you? Go home. I want to see you tonight." I told him that I would have to go to Belitze, thirty kilometers away, and that there was no transportation. I have to walk. I said, "I can't be there and back in time." He told me to bring food and supplies for a couple days, and after that I would be taken care of. Then he said, "You must return immediately to us. You belong to Mother Russia, and we'll take care of you." He said, "Come back here. From us nobody escapes! If you

drown, we'll find you drowned. If you burn, we'll find you burned."

I went home. My father and mother were scared and shocked. They worried, "What to do now?" I felt more worried for them than for myself. What should I do? My father said, "Do what your mind tells you to do and G-d should watch over you."

Even the *Istrabitilsky Battalion* were searching for me; the Russians needed to know that I was in some unit somewhere. If someone knocked on the door, I hid in my home under the bed. People came and my father told them I was in the army. Every time the door opened, I would hide. One time a girl from town came to visit my family. She was in the Russian army and she had a boyfriend, an officer in the army—a big man, an important man. My mother, father, and I were telling her this story. She said, "Maybe I can help. My friend is stationed in Vilna and he is important in his regiment. Go to Vilna and see what he can do." We decided that I should go to Vilna.[13] So I went to Vilna. She was supposed to meet me there, but I never saw her again.

On the streets of Vilna I saw two Soviet officers, a major and a colonel, standing talking. The colonel was tall and thin; the major, shorter and stocky. I walked up to them and said, "Comrades, I want to volunteer for the army." I thought to myself: "I have no choice; I am two times a deserter."

I didn't know anyone in Vilna; I had never been there before. Vilna had been destroyed quite a bit during the action between the Germans and Russians. With his hand inside his coat, the colonel asked, "Why do you want to be a soldier? Did you get tired of living?" I replied, "I am all by myself. My whole family is dead. They killed my family and friends. Everybody is dead. I want to pay them back for this." He said, "Where were you until now?" I told him, "I was in the partisans in the woods until the Russians freed us." He said, "Where were you after the partisans?" "*Istrabitilsky Battalion.*" He asked, "What went wrong over there?" I told him, "I couldn't do what I wanted to do. I decided not to be in that battalion. I want to fight. I want to do to them what they did to me."

He then saw a sergeant some distance from us and called him over. He said, "Take him for a shower and to the commissary for a uniform. After this, we'll decide where he belongs."

I felt so bad. Once I had left my family in the woods for a long time. Again I had left my family. Now I'll be sent G-d knows where.

I stayed in Vilna another three or four weeks. I made three Russian friends among the other soldiers. If one of us received a package, we would open it together and split it. My mother sent packages and rubles, which I shared with them. We were like brothers—they were non-Jews, young Russian men. They couldn't do enough for me. We had orders about keeping the room neat, clean, and spotless. They liked me and helped me do my work. There was a little cast iron coal stove in the room, and into this they put what looked to me like black stones. (We had used pieces of wood at home.) I told them that I could not light those stones and they explained that I would need kindling to start the fire and told me the black stones were coal. We got along well.

That is, except for one time: It was a military holiday celebrating the creation of the Red Army by Lenin. My three friends had gotten a bottle of vodka. They asked me to go to the kitchen to see if I could get some food. Because I knew a couple of the girls who worked in the kitchen, the cook filled my canteen with a stew of beef and potatoes. It smelled so good that on the way back I wanted to taste it, but I waited to share with my friends. We ate the stew and finished the vodka. We had a great time!

Then they said that my moustache looked like Hitler's. They said they were going to shave it. I said, "I won't let you shave it when you are drunk. I'll shave it tomorrow." However, one of them grabbed a razor and the other two held my hands behind my back. I broke away and knocked the knife out of my friend's hand and kicked it under a bunk. I then beat them up and left the room.

When I returned, they had locked the door. I could hear them inside, whispering: "Don't open the door." I kept pounding on the door until the soldier in the room opposite came out and asked me, "What is the matter?" I told him that they would not open the door. He said, "Well, you know what to do." Therefore, I broke the door down and climbed up to the top bunk, which was my bed. They complained that it was cold. I said, "Yes, the door is broken." One of them pushed the door shut and put a table in front of it to keep it closed.

Next day they went to complain to the officer about my beating them up. He questioned them, "Did this soldier beat up all three of you?" They said yes. He said, "Well, he is some soldier!"

They left and tried to find another room. I was alone in the room and did not know how to make a coal fire, so I was very cold. It was so cold that water in a

glass froze. In a few days they returned and we again were friends.

I was on the street with fellow Soviet soldiers when I saw these Germans clearing the streets. The officer I was with saw bottles in the big pockets of the Germans. He asked, "Who can speak German?" I replied, "I can." I spoke to them in Yiddish. The officer told me to tell them to take everything out of their pockets. I told them. So the German soldiers took from their pockets sealed bottles of wine and one bottle of clear liquid. This clear liquid was probably poisonous. We had been told not to eat or drink anything except what the army gave us. Day and night they announced this.

We poured out the open bottle of clear liquid and opened up the sealed bottles of wine. The officer found a little tin can in the trash, put some of the wine in this, swished it around, poured it out and then poured some more wine into the tin can. The officer told me to tell one of the soldiers to drink this. I told the soldier, "Drink it." "No," he said, "It may be poisoned." I told him." If you don't drink this, you will be kaput (dead)." He drank. He didn't die. Therefore, despite the announcements, we all started to drink from the sealed bottles of wine.

A couple of days later I developed sores on my neck and shoulders. I went to a triage unit in the street where a nurse washed me, scraped off the sores, and then put alcohol and patches on them. Next day the sores were all over my body. Then pus came out all over my body. I was very ill. Others were worse; this poison rots your body, pushing pus out from inside.

They called a surgeon, a major. He said, "What did you eat and drink?" I said, "Nothing different from what I usually eat and drink." I thought it couldn't be the wine because that was sealed. The doctor was humming an old Jewish melody. I said, "Comrade Major, are you Jewish?" He said, "No, but I was brought up among the Jews. They talked and joked with me and I learned their language. I was born among the Jews, lived among them—I am like a Jew."

I told him, "Three days ago I drank some wine, but the wine was sealed. We gave some to a German soldier to drink and he didn't drop dead." The surgeon became angry. He called me, "Stupid," and said, "You hear constantly over the loud speaker about not eating or drinking anything but what the army gives you. How many times a day are you told not to eat or drink anything?" He told me that they had injected the poison with a needle into the bottle. He said, "I can't do anything for you. What you have is a bacterial infection—from the inside, so

it does no good to treat the sores from the outside." (Penicillin was not widely available at this time, although it was used to treat wounded Allied soldiers on D-Day.) So he put me in a hospital.

I was in the hospital a long time in the section for poison, wounds, and venereal diseases. I was kept separate from other people. I saw many men who had been with me carried in on a stretcher and I saw them carried out dead on a stretcher. I got to the point where I could neither move nor swallow. Every morning, they fed me tea with a little teaspoon. Three women would carry me to the washroom to clean my wounds. Months went by.

I did get better. I was placed then in a recuperation unit. In this unit they gave me butter and sugar that I traded for cigarettes. Periodically a captain came in to check to see if we were battle ready. (The Soviet Union needed soldiers for the war against the Germans.) The captain asked, "Can he walk?" If the person could, the captain would say, "Sign him out! Sign him out!"

Chapter Nineteen
Dostavalov and the Komsomol

While I was recuperating, I made friends with a Major Dostavalov, a big man in the Communist party. He was no longer active because he had been disabled. He helped, however, in the hospital as a volunteer. He was supposed to keep the morale up among the officers—talk to them, bring them news from the front line, and generally entertain them. He organized young people to take care of the officers.

One day I met the major outside the hospital. He called me over and took out a piece of paper with a black frame around it and said, "I want to read you something. I got this dispatch from the front line. My son was killed and they sent me a copy of my son's medals." (His son had been in the army—a tank unit —and had been wounded and burned four or five times.) The major began reading the announcement to me: "Your son died as a hero for Mother Russia. His tank was blown up; only pieces of him were recovered." This was in the report. While the major was reading, tears were rolling down his face and onto his uniform. He said, "Shimenovich, would you take my son's place with me?" I felt so bad; I didn't know what to say. He invited me to his quarters. He continued, "I want you at my place tonight for dinner."

In Russia, the army food was not very good; however, officers received better food. I went to dinner and looked forward to the good food. When I arrived, I saluted. He invited me in, locked the door, and said, "You can't leave until you eat." He also said, "I don't want to see you saluting me again. When you see me on the street that is one thing." His son had been around my age—an only child. Dostavalov knew I didn't have anyone—he knew my history—the version I had told him. I was like his adopted son. I confided in him what I had told no one else. He knew that I had been in the partisans and the *Istrabitilsky Battalion*. He said that he wanted to keep me at the rehab unit as long as he could.

Dostavalov kept me from the front line. One day a captain asked me, "How long are you going to be around here? People who had come in with you and were sent to the front lines are already back in the hospital again." I replied, "I didn't come here on my own. They brought me here, and I'll leave when they sign me out." The next time I was dining with the major, I told him what had happened and what the captain had said. The major said, "And what did you tell him?" I told him what I had told the captain. The major said, "I'll tell you what I'll do: I will keep you here as long as I can. I know someone in the Recuperation Unit. I'll tell him to do the best he can to keep you there as long as he can."

Eventually Dostavalov introduced me to a Communist youth organization—*Komsomol*, the most trusted people.[14] He said, "I want you to become a member of the *Komsomol*; this is a very good thing. A very important thing." Belonging to a *Komsomol* organization was an indication that a soldier was trustworthy, was one who should set an example for others, and was one informed about many secrets about the army that the average soldier would not be aware of.

So the major recommended me to become a *Komsomol*. His recommendation was honored because he was an important person in the Communist party. At the meeting where I had to tell my past, Dostavalov sponsored me. He said, "His father was a worker, his mother, a housekeeper, and he was in the partisans, the *Istrabitilsky Battalion*, and now a volunteer in the Red Army." When he said this, everybody was applauding. They called my name to come to the front of the room: "Shimenovich." I went up and shook hands, and Dostavalov pinned a medal on me—a little flag pin with a picture of Lenin. I also got a certificate. I thought to myself, "What am I going to say?" I said the only thing I could think of: "I am serving the Soviet Union with pride." Again everybody applauded. Dostavalov said, "When they see this on you, you will be respected."

Before the meeting, Dostavalov also gave me a pistol to carry with me for my own protection; this was a present. Only officers were allowed to carry pistols. He gave me permission, but suggested that I hide the pistol. I hid the pistol in the billowy blouse of the Russian uniform. After the meeting, the major took out his pistol and fired once, and I took mine out and fired. Dostavalov—a good man!

I always wore my *Komsomol* pin and tried to be a good example to others. Sometimes soldiers were jealous of my standing in the Communist party. I was at the movies one night waiting to go in to join my buddies when three soldiers from a tank unit began to harass me. I had my jacket over my shoulders and one of the three yanked on my coat, yanking so hard that I fell back bumping hard into his nose. His nose began to bleed. He started yelling at me and punched me on the arm several times. I tried to be calm, especially because I had the *Komsomol* pin on. I told him, "One more punch and I'll let you have it." With that, he deliberately

blew blood and snot from his nose onto my shirt. I knocked him down. He called me names like "coward." A Lieutenant Katyenkova heard the ruckus and came over, saying to me, "Are you showing them an example of how a *Komsomol* should fight?" I answered, "He kept punching me. I just wanted to go to the movies and join my friends." She said, "You are going in with me." The three soldiers from the tank unit had sneaked into the movie and were sitting in the aisle. The same guy who had been punching me asked, "Are you looking for me?" She took us outside. He was mouthing off. "I won't fight you now. When I find you in the dark, I'll get you." Lieutenant Katyenkova wanted to lock me up so I would cool down. She put me in this room but I told her, "I'll go out through the window." She said, "Okay. Okay. Calm down. Calm down." I eventually calmed down. The guy was a troublemaker and I didn't want to waste any more energy on him.

While we were waiting for orders, I received a letter from my mother. Censors had blacked it all out. I could only read the bottom of the letter: "We are waiting to hear from you." I was upset. Perhaps someone was killed. I was very disturbed. My fellow soldier said, "Are you okay?" I showed him the letter and told him that I was upset because I could not read this letter. He said, "Let me see it." He went into the kitchen and soaked the paper in fat on both sides. Then he held it up to an electric bulb. I could see the writing. In the letter my parents wanted to disguise the fact that they were from Belarus. They had had documents made up that they were from Łódź—Polish citizens. My parents wrote that all the other Polish citizens had left Lida, Belarus, and that they were the only Polish family left (this was code that they were the only Jewish family left). They said that they had made up papers to go back to Poland: "Your name is on them." They wanted to hear from me.

I wanted to go to Lida but I first wanted the major to know. I thought about how and what I should say because I had told him that my parents were dead. Therefore, I went to the major very happy. I showed him the letter. He didn't read the letter. He saw the address and my mother's writing. I said, "I thought my parents had been murdered, but they weren't. My parents are alive!"

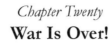

Chapter Twenty

War Is Over!

On May 9, 1945, I had more good news. The war was over!

That morning I heard shooting. I thought the Germans were coming back. I had my pistol under my pillow. I was still in my pajamas but I ran down the stairs with some others. I started moving along the side of the hospital and then realized that the shooting was coming from headquarters. I heard Russian voices. I yelled, "What is happening?" Everybody was screaming and whistling, shooting, and shouting, "The war is over! The war is over! We won the war!" They were singing and laughing, hugging each other.

The next day many flags were flying. I saw bands lined up on both sides of the road, playing military music and celebrating. Coming from the front lines were soldiers, dusty, dirty, and exhausted, straddling cannons, as if they were riding horseback, hollering, "We won the war!" Tanks were weaving in between. This went on all day. Everybody was so happy!

Chapter Twenty-One
Lida, Belarus

When the major had heard about the letter, he said, "Well, how can you leave now? You know we are staying, waiting for orders." I replied, "Comrade Major, I want just to go there and say hello and good-bye. I would like to see them." He told me that the army was waiting for transfer orders to move to Valdivostok.[15] I told him, "I'll be right back. I thought my parents were dead. I have to do what I have to do." I was sorry I had to lie to him.

He said, "Senya, I am going to be transferred to Baranavichy (Baranovichia),[16] Belarus, not far from Lida, Belarus.[17] I planned to go there to check out the city. I would like to stop in Lida to meet your parents. Indeed, as I will be transferred there, I was planning on having you with me. You would have the same uniform, but you would be my attaché (assistant of a high ranking officer, not yet an officer). What I eat; you'll eat. You'll be with me until the war is over in the Pacific. You won't have to go to Vladivostok. No front lines. When the war is over, you'll have a good life. We have everything you need. I would like to meet your parents one day. Your parents won't have to do anything. They will have the best." I believed him. He was high in the Communist party. Also I had four medals and was in the *Komsomol*.

Then he said, "Okay, I am going to send you to a friend of mine. You will have to go past the guard to get into the building. I'll send him a letter with you. I'll also call, so he'll know that you are coming for a leave of absence. They will know what this is all about." I had my *Komsomol* pin on. I went to the colonel and he said, "You may have a letter from the major; however, you know we are waiting for orders. I replied, "I want to see my family before we go to Vladivostok." He said, "I am sending you to headquarters to pick up your leave papers." I went to headquarters and they said, "We will get you your papers." You'll need documents." He told me, "Come back in three days and we'll have everything ready."

I never wore my medals. I knew medals were worthless if one had lost so many family members. A popular Russian song describes a soldier who returns home from the war and stands, looking at his wilted, overgrown garden: "All I have left is a cucumber (ugerok) and some shiny medals."

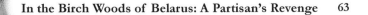

The major had introduced me to Sasha at the magazine (the warehouse) while I was in the hospital. The magazine was located next to the hospital. The major would give me an empty bottle and send me to Sasha to have it filled up. When the major and I sat down to dinner, I asked him, "What kind of drink is this?" He told me, "It's wooden alcohol that is being used in the hospital."

Among other things the magazine also stored cigarettes and rations of dry bread. I knew we had only a little food, so civilians would have less. As soon as I heard that I had to come back in three days, I made my decision not to wait for the papers and to leave right away. I went to Sasha, who gave me two handmade little wooden suitcases, as I explained to him that I was going on leave.

Cigarettes were a big item—scarce in Europe. Soldiers were given only two cigarettes a day—sometimes. Therefore, I filled one suitcase with cigarettes; the other with dried rations, mainly bread.

I took the two suitcases down to the railway station. From a distance, I saw the train starting to move slowly. By the time I got close to the train it had picked up speed. I began running like a maniac. I ran up close and threw one suitcase on the platform and then another. I next grabbed the steel handrail and jumped up, landing on the train platform. I hadn't even touched the steps. I was totally out of breath and completely exhausted. And I was scared to death.

The train was filled with soldiers but not from my outfit. So I took out a cigarette, lit it, and took a couple of puffs. (My pockets were filled with cigarettes, so I wouldn't have to go into my suitcase.) A soldier came out and asked for a few puffs. I gave him a cigarette. An officer came out and asked for a cig. I gave him one. I was scared. My uniform was from a different regiment, but I did have my *Komsomol* pin on. This gave me some comfort. However, I had no pistol and no documents. Except for the medals and the pin, I had nothing. Nothing!

We then arrived in Kovno, Lithuania.[18] In Kovno I tried to find a train going in my direction—to a town called Lida in Belarus, where my parents had moved from Belitze. This was difficult because the Lithuanians don't speak Polish, German, Russian, or Yiddish. A night watchman finally told me what train was going to Lida. The train left in the morning. I was afraid to sleep because I knew they were cutting the heads off Bolsheviks (Reds) and I was in a Russian uniform.[19] In the morning I got on the train and went to Lida.

Lida is where my parents had moved. However, I didn't know their address. I

kept asking questions and finally I found their house on a Friday. I walked up to the window and saw my father sitting with his back to the open window, eating. I said to him in Russian, "How do you feel, Dad?" My father recognized my voice immediately and said, "Oh, my G-d! Shimen is here." My mother was so happy! They were moving; this is what she had written in the letter. She said, "Our bundles of belongings are at the railroad station; we're leaving tonight."

Although I loved my family, I didn't want to leave with them. The major had promised many fine things; he had said, "When the war is over, you won't have to work a day in your life." He had said that he wanted to meet my family. I told my father that I didn't want to leave. My father took me into the marketplace where we saw a legless Russian soldier, yelling, "Kill the Jews and save Russia." My father said, "He is wearing the same uniform you are." Because of my father's concern for me and my respect for him, I decided to leave with my family and not to return to the army. This was a terrible dilemma for me.

I never saw the major again. But I still think about him and wonder what happened to him. He is in my heart. He was a wonderful man and mentor—like a father to me.

When we arrived at the station, the Russian Military Police walked up to me and said, "Are you a soldier?" I said, "Yes." Then they asked for documents. I played stupid and pulled out the certificates for my medals and showed him one. He looked at it. I gave him the second. I had the third prepared to give him; however, he didn't look at this one. He gave me back my papers, saluted and apologized, asking, "Why are you here?" I told him, "My friends, Polish citizens, are leaving. I am saying good-bye." I shook hands with my father and my mother. The military police walked one way; I walked the other way. Then I made my way back to my parents.

I only had my uniform. So my father explained to the Jewish people, who were also waiting for a train, that I had left the army and needed a suit. One man said, "I have a suit." He gave me the suit. The suit would have fit two of me. I wore it over my uniform. I was a civilian again.

We got on the train for Łódź, Poland. I threw away the *Komsomol* pin. At the border between White Russia and Poland, the N.K.V.D. came aboard with dogs (see note 12). I was shaking. Father said, "Don't show them that you are scared." They made us all get off the train while they searched it. After their

search, everything was okay, so we got back on the train, continuing on to Łódź.

In Łódź, Poland, we stopped again. The city had been destroyed. In Łódź I took off the suit. I was in uniform again. The uniform came in handy; I didn't have to stand in line. Sometimes they gave soldiers goods that other people couldn't get, but soldiers and officers could.

We stayed only briefly in Łódź. After Łódź we went through a number of cities before we arrived at a Displaced Persons' Camp (DP camp). *Brichah*, an organization that arranged illegal emigration from Soviet-occupied Europe into Allied occupied zones, helped us make our way.[20] They told us how to behave and told us to pretend to be Greeks. They even taught us a few words in Greek: "*Kalimera*" and "*Kalibera*." These words mean *good morning* and *good evening*.

While the group of twenty-five to thirty was on the train, standing in the aisle, three Russian officers were in a room in front of us. Two went to the men's room; then one came out to me. The Russian soldier happened to approach me and asked, "Where are you going?" I answered him in Greek and then in Hebrew. I figured he wouldn't know the difference. Then he let me have it. He smacked me, saying, "I help people like you, and you are afraid to tell me." He was boiling mad. Then the other two officers returned and he went back in the room with them. Later he came out and offered me a cigarette. I suppose he felt bad that he had slapped me. We finally arrived safely to Vienna and from Vienna the American trucks picked us up to transport us to a Displaced Persons (DP) Camp.

Chapter Twenty-Two

Münichholz DP Camp

From 1945 to 1952, more than 250,000 Jewish displaced persons (DPs), *Sh'erit ha-Pletah* (the surviving remnant), lived in camps and urban centers in Germany, Austria, and Italy.[21] These facilities were administered by Allied authorities and the United Nations Relief and Rehabilitation Administration—UNRRA (ushmm. org).[22]

In 1946, my family and I were in Münichholz DP Camp near Steyr, Austria, for a short time.[23] This displaced persons' camp was mostly people from the partisans and some from the army.

A guy from Hungary, Boomie, told us stories about concentration camps. This was when I first heard the stories about the death camps. I was told that Jews had been murdered and that their bodies were melted down to make soap.[24] He also told us about the lampshades that were made from people's skin. I didn't believe him. Since then, I have heard many people's experiences and knowledge of this, including my own experience that follows.

One day my brother, Richard, and I took a bus from Münichholz DP Camp to a dentist in Steyr, Austria. We had to transfer to another bus and while we were waiting, we were looking in shop windows and talking. All of a sudden I saw in the huge picture window soap stacked in a pyramid, a display of industrial soap with the initials RJF that meant *Rein Jüdisches Fett (Pure Jewish Fat)*. I said, "Richard, remember when we were talking to Boomie and he told us about that soap?" I was wild at the thought of Jewish fat having been melted down to make soap.

I was so angry that I went into the store. There were two customers in the store. I waited for my turn. When she was done with the customers, she asked me, "How can I help you?" I replied, "I want to see a piece of soap." The woman pretended that she didn't understand me. She asked, "Do you have a ration coupon." I told her, "No." But I insisted on seeing a piece of soap. She must have sensed some trouble because in no time the Austrian police with an interpreter came in. I told them, "In this soap is my mother, my father, my sisters, and brothers. I want this soap accumulated and we will come with a truck from

UNRRA and we will pick it up and take it to the Jewish cemetery to bury it—if not the whole store will fly." The interpreter tried to convince me that the soap wasn't from Jewish fat. In the midst of this, the American military police (MPs) came in. They asked me, "What is going on?" I repeated exactly what I had told the Austrian police: "In this soap is my mother, my father, my sisters, and brothers. I want to take the soap out of the window and off the shelves, and we will get a truck and take it to the Jewish cemetery and bury it—or the whole store will fly!"

The American police reassured me that everything would be taken care of. They ordered boxes and accumulated all the soap, not only from this store but from all the stores in Steyr. They took it to the Jewish cemetery, where Jews gathered, as well as rabbis from the surrounding DP camps in Austria. We said *Kaddish* (Jewish prayer for the dead). Then the soap was buried. (See Photographs section.)

Chapter Twenty-Three
More DP Camps

After Münichholz DP Camp, we were transferred to Braunau DP Camp in Upper Austria, where a highlight of my time there was performing in theatricals. Our acting group had trained in Münichholz DP Camp. Once I played an SS officer and I was so convincing that girls walking down the street, who had seen my performance, said as I passed, "He should drop dead." We performed the same play, a two-hour play about the Holocaust and the birth of Israel, in other DP camps. UNRRA had plans to send us to the United States and England but the actors left one by one, immigrating to Israel or the United States.

From Braunau DP Camp, we were transferred to Ebelsberg DP Camp in Austria. Ebelsberg was a huge camp where classes were given. The Organization for Rehabilitation through Training (ORT) gave various training courses.[25] While I was in Ebelsberg DP camp, I learned a number of skills that helped me later in life—from judo to mechanics to welding. In addition, I was trained to be a camp policeman.

When I was trained to be a chauffeur, I not only learned to drive but also I learned the mechanics of the car; so if the car broke down, the chauffeur could repair the car. This is how they did it in Europe at that time. After my training in chauffeuring and mechanics, I took my test for an International Driver's License, which I passed on the second try. I also learned welding, which meant that I learned to recognize all kinds of metals.

While I was in Ebelsberg DP camp, I was elected president of the ORT classes—an office that I did not want but that they insisted I take. I organized dances for the girls and guys to earn money for the men leaving for *Eretz Israel*[26] with the assistance of *Haganah*.[27] I tried to save coffee (which was scarce) that we received from UNRRA and sold it to area stores, earning some extra money for the people immigrating to *Eretz Israel*. I also made connections with some women, who had booths along the road, serving Coca-Cola to members of the American Army when they passed by. I was able to buy a couple cases from them. We then sold the coke and also pieces of cake at the dances that we arranged. I never charged the

men who did not have the money, however. I had a list that I gave the woman who collected the money for the cokes and cake so that these guys were not charged.

When the men left for Israel via Italy, they had money in their pockets and they went off with our prayers that they would not be killed by the British before their arrival in Israel.[28]

One day the Haganah *group came to our apartment on the third floor of the building. My father welcomed them. Then they tried to get my brother, Richard, and me to go with them to Eretz Israel. My father said, "Sure, they can go but I, too, am going." They told him that he could come later. My father told them, "They are not going without me." Then the* Haganah *threatened my father. But my father was a strong man and he told them, "If you come back here, I'll throw you out the window." They never bothered us again.*

Chapter Twenty-Four
Immigration to the United States

While we were in Ebelsberg near Linz, Austria, my father's brother, Uncle Joe Simon, who lived in the United States found out that we were alive. He wrote my father that we should come to the US—to Baltimore, Maryland. He sent the family documents; however, he didn't know our birth dates so he made them up. *To this day some of my documents have January 1, 1925, the birth date my uncle gave me.*

My uncle came to the United States long before World War II. Josef would send my *Bubbe* (grandmother) shoes; he didn't realize that my mother had a store full of shoes—better ones. As a child I remember a letter Josef had sent to my father, telling him to immigrate to the United States—the *goldene medina*. My father had answered his brother, writing, "I have it better than America right here." And he did! Until the Germans came, that is.

I was hesitant about going to the United States because I had met a girl, Shulamit, in Ebelsberg DP Camp, in Austria, and I didn't want to leave her. Shulamit couldn't go to the United States because her sister had something wrong with her lungs—perhaps tuberculosis. But Israel would accept the sister. Therefore, her mother and sister were going to Israel, as was Shulamit. We were supposed to be married. My idea was to go to Israel. I wanted to go. My father said, "If you go and you starve, I will know nothing about it." Father said, "If she means more to you than us, go!"

I didn't go to Israel. The papers came though for the United States, and my name was on them. The family boarded a train and went to Bremerhaven, a port in the north of Germany. There were father, mother, Richard, Katie, Katie's husband Isaac, Katie's daughter Charlotte, Ida, and Ida's husband, Shunek.

When we left Bremerhaven, Germany, the officer asked me, "What is your name?" I answered, "Shimenovich." The woman repeated, "Shimenovich! My G-d! How do you spell that?" I wrote my name for her. She asked, "Where are you going?" I replied, "To Baltimore." "Who will meet you?" "My uncle." "What is his name?" "Simon," I said. She said, "Fine. Simon is good enough." So that was my uncle's name. And it is our name also.

We sailed March 26, 1949, on the *USS Marine Flasher*.[29]

What am I doing in America? I am not sorry that I didn't go to Israel. I am happy here with Rosalie and my family.

Chapter Twenty-Five
Baltimore

On Passover, April 13, 1949 (5709), my family and I arrived in Boston and were put on military trucks, bringing us to Baltimore, Maryland. My uncle had everything prepared for us—an apartment that had a cellar full of canned goods for us. So we had the apartment, canned goods, and $20.00 that we had borrowed from a man on board the ship; he knew us because he had been a butcher in the DP camp. Within weeks, from the first money we made, we sent what we had borrowed back to the man, living in New York.

We had jobs waiting. The day after we arrived we were working. All of us worked hard and contributed our earnings to the family.

I missed my girlfriend. We wrote back and forth to each other. I wanted to go to Israel. In 1948, Israel had become a country. My uncle introduced me to a Zionist organization, which encouraged immigration to Israel; I went to their meetings. I registered in a group to immigrate to Israel. In the meantime I worked.

Because I didn't speak English, my uncle got me my first job, at a factory making Sweetheart Cups. Mr. Shapiro, the factory owner, had factories all over the United States, making straws, ice cream cones, and machinery. In fact, he had donated a factory to Israel. He had a factory in France as well. He liked me because he saw that I was a hard worker. My foreman on the factory floor spoke Yiddish with me.

In those days the cups had a hot wax coating so the area around the machines was very hot. One day the man's machine next to mine broke in a jagged split. My foreman, who knew I could weld, asked me to repair the other man's machine. I objected because I was roasting hot, and I didn't want to become even hotter from the welding and also because it wasn't my machine that was broken. I just wanted to continue working. After this the foreman would not speak Yiddish to me—only English that I had trouble understanding. That Friday I received two checks. I thought I had gotten a raise. The Spanish girls who packed the cups into boxes explained through sign language that I had been fired. I didn't know what this "fire" meant. They explained, yelling, "Go. Go." I couldn't believe it. I asked the foreman why I was fired, but he would only respond in English, which I could not understand.

Then I went to Mr. Shapiro and asked why I had been fired. He explained in Yiddish that he had been watching my work and would have one day put me in charge of a factory because he had many factories throughout the United States. However, the best he could do for me now was to give me a job in one of his other factories, a factory that made ice cream cones.

So the next Monday I started at the cone factory. This was a horrible job—hot and tedious. In front of me was a metal cone over which batter, the consistency of pancake batter, flowed. I wore two gloves on each hand because the metal became so hot. I had to push flat pancakes into the oven, one at a time, and the machine would make the pancake into a cone. Pancake after pancake after pancake! Very boring! And the repetitive motion was hard on my arm. After several months, I gave the foreman an excuse so I could take a week off—I told him my family was taking a vacation. He said that he couldn't promise that my job would be there when I returned. I didn't care. I wasn't coming back.

I did, however, remain good friends with Mr. Shapiro, sometimes consulting with him for advice.

Chapter Twenty-Six

The Concrete Company

I then got a job at a company owned by a man named Meyerhof, very prominent in Baltimore, Maryland. We stayed in Meyerhof's house in Baltimore. My mother was hired by one of his sons, Jack, and in return for rent my mother took care of his old mother, who was ill and unable to take care of herself. My job was in his concrete and gravel business. I replaced two people. I watched the conveyor belt that took the gravel to be washed. I had to watch this belt so only the correct sized gravel went into the cement mixer. If there were any stones, that is, bigger than the gravel pieces, I had to pick them out or the belt would jam. The conveyor belt never stopped, except at lunchtime.

At lunch time everything stopped. Then the foreman, Homer, a German-American, and the others had lunch together. Homer didn't care for Jews. Mr. Duncan in the office was a good human being; he was nice to me. The others were like Homer. I had tried to eat with them but couldn't. One time they called me over to show me photographs of Jews forced to have sex on the streets in Germany. Homer was showing these photos to the others. Another time he showed me a photograph of a rabbi having his beard burned off. Homer thought this was funny. All the others were laughing. I walked away. A little later Homer fired me. My mother told the owner, Meyerhof. He said, "I can't fire all the others because of Sidney. I need them."

One time when I was still working for Meyerhof, I saw a crane with a sign on it—Osgood Company. (I was reading signs by this time.) Homer was behind me when I was reading. He said, "I know damn well that you will not be working here too long.

Chapter Twenty-Seven

Plumber's Helper

My next job was as a plumber's helper on a big project, building homes in the suburbs of Baltimore, for Max Kleinman, the plumbing contractor for the entire development. The foreman on the job was Mr. Kleinman's son-in-law Michael. The plumber mechanic that I was helping was called Junior.

Our goal as a pair, the helper and plumber, was to finish ¾ of a house each day, putting in plumbing upstairs and downstairs. I worked hard with Junior and we would finish very quickly. Everyday during our lunch break I would have the same sandwich as Junior. Junior would say, "I am having such and such a sandwich. Sidney, what are you going to have?" I would say, "The same." These were some English words that I knew. So I'd have the same sandwich as Junior and with that a bottle of milk. Most days the foreman, Michael, would go by, and because he knew my name, he would say, "Shake a leg, Sidney. Sidney, get up." Mike knew he could harass me and get me back to work and the other guys would follow. I couldn't argue with him because my English was not yet good enough. I didn't know what Mike was saying, but Junior did. One day Junior got sick of Mike and his remarks. He took one of those huge wrenches and said, "Mike, so help me G-d, I'll knock you down dead, if you don't stop bothering Sidney. You know that he is doing the work of two people."

Mike took me off that job with Junior and gave me my own young kid for a helper. The problem was that I couldn't tell my helper what to do to help me because he only spoke English. So I told him, "Sit." I didn't know many English words yet. I couldn't tell him what to do, so I did the work. I could carry a cast iron tub up to the second floor by myself. And the stairs weren't completed! There were only the risers. I would put my head into the tub and carry it up balanced on my body. I would then figure the elevation, cut the pipe, rim the pipe, and thread the pipe all by myself. I did a house a day! All by myself! Better than ¾ of a house!

One day my father saw me with my shirt off and he was surprised, saying to me, "Oy! Oy! Look at this!" I thought, "What does he mean? What is it?" He commented on my well-muscled body, a result of all the heavy lifting associated with my plumbing job.

Mike continued to harass me on the job and that made Junior furious. One Friday, Junior told me in front of Mike, "Sidney, when Mike goes to pick up the parts for tomorrow, go with him and ask Mr. Kleinman for a raise." Later on Junior told me, when Mike was not present, "If you don't get a raise, I'll take you to a place where I used to work and I am sure you will get more money for the work you are producing."

Friday after work, I followed Mike to the office. Mr. Kleinman asked Mike, "Is Sidney with you?" Mike replied, "No." Then Mr. Kleinman asked me, "What can I do for you, Sidney?" I told him, "I would like to have a raise." He said, "Do you know what a raise means?" I answered, "Yes, more money." He said, "When I came to America, I didn't make this kind of money. See. I am trying to make a man out of you." I apologized, and I left.

I never went back.

Chapter Twenty-Eight
Scrap Metal

On that same Friday, on the way home, I was passing by a huge place called United Iron and Metal Company.[30] I decided to stop in to see if I could get a job as a metal sorter. I knew metals because in the DP camp I had gone to the ORT school to learn welding (see Chapter 23). That is how I was acquainted with all kinds of metals and the alloys. The foreman, Mr. Bundy, a German Jew, asked me, "Do you know metals?" I said, "Yes."

Mr. Bundy took me in front of barrels of different kinds of metals and questioned me. I gave him all the correct answers, and I was hired. I stayed there until I had learned the names of the metals in English—about ten days. I liked the job. I was treated well. But I had the desire to start for myself.

I talked this over with my father and my brother, Richard, and we decided among us to give it a try. Richard was working as a plumber's helper at the time. Richard and I formed a partnership by the name of Simon Brothers Scrap Metal. Between my father, brother, and me we had saved up $2000.00 from our earnings. While still on the job on our day off, for the $2000.00, Richard and I had bought a truck and all the necessary equipment to get started in the scrap metal business for ourselves.

On Friday, I went to get my check from the cashier. After she handed me my pay check, I told her that I wanted the money they had been holding—three days or so. She told Mr. Bundy that I was leaving. He told the boss and then said to me, "The boss wants to see you." The boss's name was Mr. Shapiro, another Shapiro, not related. In Yiddish, Mr. Shapiro asked me, "Is anyone mistreating you? Aren't you satisfied with your pay?" I then explained to him that I wanted to go into business for myself. I told him, "I bought the equipment, Mr. Shapiro." Mr. Shapiro said, "I'll take all the equipment that you bought. I'll give you the money. I will let you work piece work. Whatever metal you sort, I will pay you for each sort."

I said, "No, I'm sorry. I want to start on my own." He responded, "My doors are always open to you. I'll double the wages or pay you piece work." I thought,

"A very generous offer." However, I was determined to be on my own.

Months went by. Nothing. No business. No money for gas or a sandwich. My brother, Richard, who had been working with me said, "I am going to get a job." I told him, "I am not giving up." I continued on my own. I tried very hard to contact various machine shops, asking them to sell their scrap metal to me, but they already had their own people whom they were dealing with, and I was constantly refused. As I had mentioned, I was working previously for Meyerhof Sand and Gravel Company. I remembered there was a gravel pit where they used to dump all kinds of junk, such as steel, old chains from bulldozers, and a lot of other old equipment. I decided to go there to see if I could buy this junk. I knew that I could sell this metal and make a profit. Luckily I was able to make a deal with them. I sold the metal with a nice profit. That was my first break in this business.

Business continued at a slow pace until one day I happened to stop on Pulaski Highway in Baltimore to a machine shop by the name of Joseph J. Martin and Company. I met with Mr. Martin, the owner. I introduced myself, explaining who I was and where I came from. He knew that I was not American-born by my limited English. I asked him to give me a chance by selling his scrap metal to me. I also told him that I would weigh it in his presence, so he would not have any doubts as to the amount of weight. For some reason, he trusted me and sold his scrap metal to me. Eventually we established a friendship, and I was the only one he was dealing with for scrap metal. He belonged to a club with other machine shop owners who were his friends. He told them about me, and as a result of his convincing them of my trustworthiness, they were also willing to deal with me— one by one, in time, they came to me. This was a huge help to me. Mr. Martin also tried to get me into Black and Decker but that was the only machine shop I could not get. They were obligated to someone else. I owe Mr. Martin a lot.

I did well. People were good to me.

Chapter Twenty-Nine
Rosalie

In 1950 I was struggling to make my scrap metal business prosperous in Baltimore. I was attending evening school on Smallwood Avenue in Baltimore. I was learning the English language there. I started up a conversation with a young woman by the name of Helen Lebovitch. She seemed to be very nice, so I offered to drive her home. She accepted; however, when she found out that she was about two years older than I, she suggested that she introduce me to her two younger sisters, Rajzi and Rosalie. After I had met them, I called my friend Sol, told him about the two sisters, and asked him if he wanted to double date with me. He agreed. I took out Rosalie and he took out Rajzi. We went in separate cars, and I agreed to meet Sol at the end of the evening. I had an old Buick jalopy, so Rosalie and I went out in that. We went to a park. A movie or dinner was a luxury I couldn't afford. We talked, but the evening was not a success.

When Sol and I met at the end of the evening, I asked Sol if he had a good time. He said, "Yes." I confided to Sol that I had tried to kiss Rosalie but she had slapped me. I thought that Rosalie and I were over. But I tried again. She was eighteen years old when I met her and according to what she told me later she was quite influenced by the American movies that she had watched, as a teenager, in Czechoslovakia after the war. Some of the movie stars slapped their boy friends when they were kissed. Rosalie laughed at her naiveté and told me that she had done the same thing to a boy she had dated in Czechoslovakia (he later became Chief of Pediatrics in a hospital in Chadera, Israel). Rosalie apologized and never slapped me again for kissing her.

Eventually we grew to love each other, and married on June 1, 1952. (By then Sol and Rajzi were married.)

We were married in my parents' home, surrounded by relatives and a few friends. My mother cooked the food and baked some cookies. She was an excellent cook.

After we married, we moved into a small one bedroom, furnished apartment—an upstairs one. We had no air-conditioning. Rosalie's dowry was a down bed pillow.

I went to work the next day. I worked hard to make a better life for Rosalie and me. She stayed near the telephone, answering my business calls. Rosalie soon became pregnant with our first child.

We've been married for fifty-six years—as of 2008. I thank G-d every day for having Rosalie in my life.

Chapter Thirty
The Farm in Pleasantville

Before Rosalie and I were married, we had gone to Atlantic City for a weekend. We stayed with Joe Lifshin, brother of my sister-in-law, Betty, who was married to my brother, Richard. Joe knew that I had a scrap metal business in Baltimore. But Joe was a chicken farmer, and he suggested that I buy a farm and then my father would have it easier.[31]

My father was then working as a carpenter in Baltimore, and going and coming, to and from his job, he had to transfer buses every day. His English was not very good, so he had memorized landmarks and then he would know where to get off the buses. One landmark he knew was a boat at a shipyard. However, one day the boat sailed, and my father, not seeing this landmark, became lost. Not being fluent in English made life very difficult for him when he was traveling back and forth.

Joe took me to the agent who had sold him his farm. The agent had no farm available at that time, but he had a piece of land that was suitable for a farm. The land was located on Route 9 in Pleasantville; the property had a house on it. After seeing the property, we went back to Joe Lifshin's house. He asked me, "How did you like it?" I told Joe, "I liked it, but it is not up to me. My father has to like it because he will be living there. When I go home, I'll talk to my father and get back to you."

After returning to Baltimore, I explained to my father what I had seen. I told him, "Joe Lifshin said to me that he is very happy living on a farm. Also he said that there are quite a few newcomers in the surrounding area." My father thought it was a great idea, but he said, "I have no money." I told him, "All I want to know is if you like the idea? I will take care of the rest." So I provided the money to buy the land. My father and brother, Richard, went to Joe Lifshin, who took them to the agent and they made settlement.

My father, brother Richard, and Betty moved into the house. My mother was still in Baltimore because Mrs. Meyerhof was still alive and needed my mother's care. After I married, my sister, Ida, her husband, Shunek, and daughter, Lillian,

three years old, moved in with my mother. After Mrs. Meyerhof died, mother came to the farm. Ida, her husband, Shunek, and Lillian moved out of the house and bought a little grocery store in Dundalk, Maryland.

After settlement was made, purchasing the land for the farm, money was needed to build the chicken coops. I went to my friend, Sol Miller, who was my brother-in-law, the husband of Rajzi, Rosalie's sister, and got a loan from him. I was very close with him. He never refused me. I told him, "As I make money, I will pay you back." And I did.

Subsequently, every time money was needed on the farm, my father called me, and I delivered the money in person. Richard and my father worked on the farm and in addition they hired a man to help feed the 7,000 layers and collect the eggs. My father, Richard, and I were partners. Richard contacted restaurants, diners, and grocery stores, where he delivered the eggs. The money from egg sales contributed towards the on-going expenses of the farm. The money I made from the scrap metal business went to pay off the debts.

Chapter Thirty-One

Atlantic City

In Baltimore, I continued working in my scrap metal business. My business was growing and so was my family. We had a son—Majshe (Mitchell), born in 1953, named after my brother. He was beautiful but he had eczema, a very bad case. We took him to Johns Hopkins Hospital as an outpatient. They gave us creams to put on him, but these made his whole scalp raw—oozing. Nothing worked. They said, "There is nothing more we can do for him. However, we could try some experimental drugs on him." I said, "No, my baby is not a guinea pig." We didn't want them to experiment on Mitchell.

It was heartbreaking for Rosalie and me to watch our baby in such discomfort. In the summer I would come home from a hard day at work and I would go in to see Mitchell in his crib. Although his little hands were covered to prevent him from scratching, he still managed to rub his face and neck until he was bleeding. His skin would crack from the heat and lack of air. It was so hot that Rosalie would hold him near the windowsill so he could get some air. On top of everything, Rosalie was confined to the house, taking messages for me on behalf of my business. (There were no answering machines.)

Then my Uncle Joe told us about a skin specialist in Atlantic City—a Dr. Klein, on Pacific Avenue. We went to Dr. Klein. After examining Mitchell, Dr. Klein suggested that Rosalie and Mitchell stay in the area for a week for the baby to be treated.

Dr. Klein said, "Leave Mitchell nearby for a week." Rosalie said to me, "What about the telephone?" She was my right hand on the telephone. I said, "We have to give Mitchell this chance." So Rosalie and the baby stayed on the farm on New Road in Pleasantville, and I went back to Baltimore. Because Rosalie was not available for that week to answer the telephone calls, this created a problem as each machine shop usually called me when the scrap metal needed to be picked up so it would be out of their way. After I discussed my situation with the owners, they understood and went along with me.

I came back to Atlantic City on Saturday and went to the farm. I asked

Rosalie, "How's Mitchell?" She said, "Go look at him." I couldn't believe it. Dr. Klein had put Mitchell under fluorescent lights with protective glasses on his eyes. The salt air had also helped to cure our baby. Rosalie said, "Dr. Klein suggested that we move to the Atlantic City area, so that Mitchell will continue to be near the salt air of the ocean."

I didn't know what to do. My business was established and I was making good money. Furthermore, it was not a business that I could sell. I hired someone to help me, but I didn't like this. I didn't think he was doing a good job. However, my scrap metal customers were very understanding. Mr. Peterson, especially, who had Scandia Manufacturing Company, became my friend for life.

Later after I moved to Pleasantville, he called me at my office and said, "Sidney, I want to have lunch with you?" I answered, "How will you get here? You're in Baltimore; I'm here in Atlantic City." Pete said, "I'll fly there, Sidney. I have my own plane. Pick me up at Bader Field Airport in Atlantic City."[32] *Pete flew in especially to have lunch with me. We invited Peterson to Mitchell's* Bar Mitzvah, *and he replied that he was honored to be invited, and he came. We, in turn, were invited to his daughter's wedding.*

However, gradually I gave up my business in Baltimore.

Chapter Thirty-Two
The Family on the Farm

Rosalie and I made a decision to relocate from Baltimore to the Atlantic City area for the sake of Mitchell's well-being and upon the recommendation of Dr. Klein. We moved to the farm in 1954. Rosalie, Mitchell, and I lived in the same house with mother, father, Richard, Betty, and their little girl, Marcia. The house was two-stories with a cellar where we candled the eggs.[33] We worked hard to make the house comfortable.

One day one of the workers was replacing a windowpane. He removed the broken glass and placed this in a box. Mitchell, who was three years old, was running around the house, as kids will do. He fell into the box and the jagged pieces of glass cut him terribly on the knee and stomach. In fact, the glass went up through his knee, thigh, and into his abdomen. I wasn't home, so my brother, Richard, took Mitchell and Rosalie to the hospital. Rosalie had to carry him because he could not walk. It was a long time before Mitchell healed.

I wasn't there to take Mitchell to the hospital because I was rarely home then. I was still trying to run my scrap metal business in Baltimore.

Then in September of 1956, our daughter, Ruthie, was born. Rosalie loved Ruthie very much. But she became more and more depressed. Perhaps Rosalie was suffering from post-partum depression, but they didn't call it that then.[34] Rosalie used to cry all the time, and one time I saw her outside—just lying there, crying. Fortunately, Ruthie was a good baby; she lay in her crib happily. So Rosalie stayed in bed a lot, but she would get up when Ruthie cried for her. Rosalie lost weight; she couldn't eat. I took her out to a restaurant and she couldn't eat.

I was not in good health either. At this time I was 5' 11" but only weighed 145 pounds. My doctor told me that I had to change my life style—I was still going back and forth, from Pleasantville to Baltimore and back. I saw how depressed Rosalie was. I wanted to get out of the farm. I knew I could do other things. Richard also wanted out. So I bought Richard out and eventually left the farm to my father.

We stayed on the farm until we rented a house in 1958, on Marion Avenue,

in Pleasantville. We moved to Margate in 1962; I had bought a lot there and we had a home built. In 1967, our younger son, William, was born. William is named after Rosalie's brother who was murdered during the *Shoah*.[35]

Chapter Thirty-Three
Other Ventures

When I came to Pleasantville, in addition to the chicken farm, I had a roadside stand with fresh chickens, eggs, fruits, and vegetables, and I was also into government surplus. The surplus came from a military base located in Chambersburg, Pennsylvania.

I would rent a piece of land—two acres—where vegetables or melons were already grown. Then I would harvest them and sell them at my roadside stand. After this, I bought surplus pick up trucks, jeeps, and tires. I also unintentionally bid on a blind lot; I rubbed my nose and they accepted this as my bid. I sent a truck to pick the lot up, and I discovered I had bid on surplus Eisenhower jackets— brand new, and I bought them very cheap.[36] I hung those Eisenhower jackets on the stand and sold them along with the fruits and vegetables. I also fixed up old cars—five or six at a time—and sold them used to young guys from the naval base in Pomona, New Jersey. I was still dealing with business in Baltimore, too.

As time passed I got heavier into government surplus. Frank Garafola became my partner. We bid on tires for our first venture together. Frank knew tires so I took him with me to an army base in Raritan, New Jersey, so he could check them out. We bought them and before we were even home someone on the road offered us a price for them. I wouldn't take the offer. We sold them separately at Frank's gas station on Doughty Road and the Blackhorse Pike. We made a profit.

Another time we bought and sold surplus Army GMC trucks—heavy-duty trucks, ten wheelers. Eventually we became South Jersey Automotive and Equipment Company, and Charley Price came in on the business. We would go to sales all over. All the dealers called us the Three Musketeers. Then we spread out buying from other military bases—Aberdeen Proving Grounds, Philadelphia Naval Base, Raritan Arsenal, Schenectady Army Base, and Fort Dix. We shipped parts as far away as Argentina, South America.

Later I went into land developing—always a good investment. We had three sub-divisions in Cumberland County, New Jersey, and two in Egg Harbor Township.

I was on the radio advertising my business in Washington, Newark, Philadelphia, and Baltimore.

I did well. Sometimes there would be a cash flow problem, but overall my ventures were successful and I have made a good living. But more importantly, I have tried to be a good man—an ethical businessman.

I made it easy for people to buy land in my developments; I sold lots that they could buy on time. Indeed, I have heard people say, "Thank G-d for Mr. Simon. I wouldn't have property if it weren't for him." If a family was behind in the payments, I always waited until the family could resume the payments. I never repossessed the land. I always gave customers the chance.

I remember one day my son Mitchell and I were sitting in my office with a man and his son, Mitchell's age. The father had bought land—beautiful plots—for himself and for the son. He was far behind on his payments, so they had to come to the office. The man and his son were crying because they didn't want to lose the land. Mitchell could not bear watching the two cry. He walked out of the office. He then called me out, saying, "Dad, I want to show you something." When I came out, Mitchell said, "How could you see this—a son watching his father cry? Give him the land." Mitchell felt sorry for this man. So although I did not "give" the man the land, I made it easier for him to make his payments. We were all happy—the man and his son, of course, and Mitchell and I. I was very proud of the compassion that Mitchell had shown.

Chapter Thirty-Four

Return to Belitze

In the late 1980s, Rosalie and I together with my brother, Richard, and sister-in-law, Betty took a trip to Belitze. We also visited many other places and beautiful sights, among them Moscow, The Hermitage in Leningrad, and Minsk where I still had relatives. We had a great time together. I miss Richard, who died in 2005, and as I look back in my life, I appreciate all the special times we shared.

The second time we went to Belitze in July 1999, again with Richard and Betty, included my son William, my nieces Marcia, Renee, Valerie, Lillian, and Charlotte and Lillian, and Charlotte's children, Erica and Peter. We were joined by a group of other people from the United States and Israel. Unfortunately, my sister, Ida, was not able to take the trip as she was taking care of her husband, Shunek, who was ill at the time. We really missed her being there.

In Belitze and the surrounding towns we visited many memorial monuments and mass graves where countless Jewish people and children were buried—killed by the Nazis. Among them was the monument where the rabbi of Belitze was tortured and murdered along with thirty-five other Jews. Kaddish was recited at each grave while we stood there silently with tears in our eyes mourning the dead. Although the events of the day remained painfully in our hearts, in the evenings we all got together for dinner, and often to lighten their hearts the young people sang and danced.

Sometimes we think that the Holocaust has only affected Holocaust survivors and their children. On both trips to Belitze I was reminded that the Holocaust has also affected perpetrators and their children. To explain this I have to go back to the time of the ghettoization of Belitze's Jews:

In our town, a shoemaker—he made the uppers—named Sheshko, and his family had made a good living before 1941, the year the Germans occupied Belitze. But in early 1942, when the Jews were sent to the Žetel Ghetto, Sheshko and his family left everything they had with their neighbor, Kulesh, a Christian friend. This friend said that he would take good care of the family's possessions, keeping them safe until the war ended.

One time the neighbor, Kulesh, came to the Sheshkos in the ghetto and offered the whole family poison pills. He told them to take the pills so that they would not be tortured to death. Sheshko said he would not take the pill and neither would anyone else in his family.

When the Germans made the Żetel Ghetto Judenrein, *the Sheshkos escaped to the home of their Christian neighbor, Kulesh. He said, "Yes, I will hide you and your family in my stable. I will feed you. And after the war, you will be freed." While the family hid in the stable, their friend rode on horseback to the Germans and reported them. The Germans came and captured the family. They took them near the church where there was a huge area of vacant land. There they tortured and shot the whole family.*

When I was in the partisans, we knew about this man. One night a group of partisans came to Kulesh's house, ostensibly asking him for directions to a certain place. They ordered him to get dressed and to take them to the place where they wanted to go. Kulesh said he would show them the way. When they came to the River Neman, they took Kulesh onto the cable ferry (a boat pulled from shore to shore by a cable and wench set-up) and pulled the ferry into the middle of the River Neman. Then the partisans beat him up, gouging out his eyes. After this, they took rocks, attaching them to both his feet, and tied his hands behind his back before dropping him in the river.

When we were back to Belitze the second time, Rosalie, the rest of the group, and I went to visit the Jewish cemetery. We saw an older man in a horse and wagon with milk cans on the back, taking the cans to a central depot for processing. I stopped him and asked him for directions to the cemetery. He said, "I live near the cemetery. Follow me." We followed him to the cemetery, introducing ourselves.

After we had visited the cemetery, we saw the man come out of his house and he approached us. He said, "I am Kulesh's son. Many years ago Jewish partisans came and took my father away because they thought he had reported the Sheshko family to the Germans. This is not so! Another neighbor saw the Jewish family, and that neighbor reported them to the Nazis. But the partisans took my father away. I don't even know where his bones are. I have one question for you. I heard that one of Sheshko's sons is alive. Do you know if Hyme Sheshko is alive?"

I said, "Sure. He's alive." He said, "Where is he?" I replied, "In the United States. I see him occasionally." *Hyme is not alive; however, I wanted the son to worry about Hyme's revenging his father.* So even fifty and more years after the Holocaust, the evil that people did still affects their families.

After we had talked to him, he went inside. A little later an older woman, the wife of Kulesh's son, came out of the same house near the cemetery. We watched

her and she went to a garden she had planted in the cemetery. She was picking cucumbers. I asked her, "Do you know these are graves? Do you have permission to plant here?" She said, "I am part of a cooperative. I don't know from nothing." I told her, "I'll tell the Russians what you are doing."

After the Jews from Belitze were destroyed and their culture vanished, this non-Jewish woman still had no respect for the Jewish dead, desecrating the graves in the Jewish cemetery. She and her husband seem only to worry about what they have lost not about what their neighbors lost in that time of terror.

However, many in Belitze did welcome us, greeting us with *challah* (braided bread, traditionally eaten for the Sabbath meal) and salt, the symbols of welcome. (See Photographs section.)

Chapter Thirty-Five
Epilogue

Today Rosalie and I are retired and enjoying life in New Jersey. Our greatest joy is our children and our grandchildren. We are blessed.

As I reflect on my life, growing up in a small village surrounded by family and friends, I am wondering what my life would have been like had I not been faced with a war.

I attended school and enjoyed all the activities boys at that time took part in. At the age of fourteen, I left home and went to another town, Žaludek, to learn a trade. Because there was only one barbershop in my town, I thought I could make a nice living being a barber.

We don't know what life has in store for us, but most likely I would have spent my life as a barber in Belitze. However, my life was turned upside when the Germans invaded our territory. Witnessing all the horrors perpetrated by the Nazis turned me into a different person; I was no longer a carefree boy. I was deeply affected by what I had witnessed.

What I did during the war was because of the rage I carried inside me. I did what I thought was right for me. I have no regrets.

Educating the world about the Holocaust is most important. Perhaps it will diminish the prejudice and hatred that still exist. My hope for future generations is that, in time, all races and all religions will be able to live in peace.

Peace in this universe is everything.

JFS Dedicates Rosalie and Sidney Simon Wall of Honor

The JFS Wall of Honor, at the Samuel and Czerna Simon Jewish Family Service Building on Jerome Avenue was dedicated in honor of Sidney and Rosalie Simon.

Dr. Mitchell Simon, one of Sidney and Rosalie Simon's sons, spoke on behalf of the family at the dedication, which was attended by a hundred people. The Wall of Honor features the original artwork of ChoraLeone Art and Design Group of Egg Harbor Township. It also lists the names of those who have contributed to the Building Fund for the new building as well as the JFS Fund, which is the agency's endowment fund.

The dedication was the culmination of a three year process that witnessed the complete renovation of the old Hebrew Academy Building into a modern headquarters for this growing social service agency. . . . .

"We are so grateful to Rosalie and Sidney Simon for their support of our new building and to all the people who participated in the Building Fund so that we will be able to maintain this wonderful facility in the future," said JFS President Ken Steinberg at the dedication.

—*Jewish Times of South Jersey* 8.4, January 23, 2004, page 1.

Endnotes

[1] **Belarus** "After the Polish-Soviet War ended in 1921, Byelorussian lands were split between Poland and the recreated Byelorussian SSR, which became a founding member of the Union of Soviet Socialist Republics in 1922. In September 1939, the Soviet Union annexed the Polish-held Byelorussian land as a result of the Molotov-Ribbentrop Pact.

In 1941, Nazi Germany launched *Operation Barbarossa*, invading the Soviet Union. Belarus was captured soon afterwards, and remained in Nazi hands until 1945. Much of the country was destroyed and much of its population was killed in the German invasion. The Jewish population of Belarus was also devastated during the Holocaust."--www.wikipedia.com

[2] **Neman River** "The Neman River is a major European river rising in Belarus and flowing through Lithuania before draining into the Baltic Sea near Klaipėda. It is the 14th largest river in Europe, 1st largest in Lithuania, and the 3rd largest in Belarus. The largest cities on the Neman are Hrodna (Belrus), Alytus and Kaunas (Lithuania), and Sovetsk (Russia)."—www.wikipedia.com

[3] **Jewish tavern owners** "Until 1910, all of the tavern keepers were required to receive a permit from the governor of the city, as were all places of business. In 1910 a law was issued, which was ratified in parliament due to pressure from the Polish anti-Semites, which required all taverns to be overseen by the Austrian ruler. This was opposite of the situation in Bohemia and Moravia, where the Jewish population was small, and the majority of the taverns were owned by Christians. The influence of this new law was very great in Galicia. In Rzeszow, the Jewish tavern keepers, who were 90% of the tavern keepers, presented requests to the authorities; however, 30% of the concessions were given to Christians. In the demonstration of Jewish tax collectors, which took place in Vienna with over 2,000 participants, letters of request were presented to Kaiser Franz Josef I and members of parliament. After the large demonstration, the government increased the number of concessions that were granted to Jews" —www.jewishgen.org/yizkor/rzeszow

[4] **Birth Date** On many of my documents my birth date is shown as January 1, 1925. When my Uncle Joe Simon was preparing the documents for my

family so we could immigrate to the United States, he just made up birth dates for all of the children.

   [5] **Nazi-Soviet Pact** "The Molotov-Ribbentrop Pact, also known as the Hitler-Stalin Pact or Ribbentrop-Molotov Pact or Nazi-Soviet Pact and formally known as the *Treaty of Nonaggression between Germany and the Union of Soviet Socialist Republics,* was in theory a non-aggression treaty between the German Third Reich and the Soviet Union. It was signed in Moscow on August 23, 1939, by the Soviet foreign minister Vyacheslav Molotov and the German foreign minister Joachim von Ribbentrop. The mutual non-aggression treaty lasted until *Operation Barbarossa* of June 22, 1941, when Nazi Germany invaded the Soviet Union.

   Although officially labelled a "non-aggression treaty," the pact included a secret protocol, in which the independent countries of Finland, Estonia, Latvia, Lithuania, Poland, and Romania were divided into the spheres of interest of the [two countries]. The secret protocol explicitly assumed *'territorial and political rearrangements'* in the areas of these countries, which practically rendered it into an aggressive military alliance, in spite of its official name. Subsequently all the mentioned countries were invaded by either the Soviets, the Nazis, or both. Only Finland, which fought twice against the Soviet Union in WWII, successfully resisted conquest, but was forced to concede territory."—en.wikipedia.org

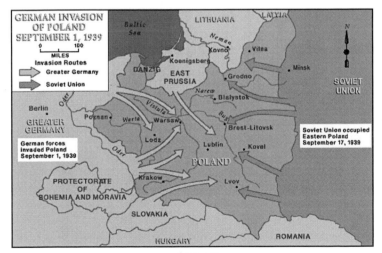

ushmm.org

⁶ Shoes Because we have available to us so many inexpensive shoes, we may not realize the value of shoes in other times and places. Shoes back then were very valuable, often handcrafted. Mojshe's mother gave him something valuable when he left for the east. The shoes could be bartered, if need be. See also note 9.

⁷ Dvoretsky, Alter *The Underground in the Zhetel [Žetel] Ghetto* (Shalom Gerling in *Pinkes Zhetel*, p. 372; translation, A. Patt)

"The initiative behind the underground in Zhetel, its organizer and spirit was the attorney, **Alter Dvoretsky**. A lot of courage and effort was required, in order to undertake under those conditions, the activities of an underground. These efforts required extreme caution on three levels: in the face of the Germans, the local Christian population, and before a majority of the Jewish population, who were opposed to acts of violence, which they believed could endanger the well-being of the ghetto.

The unfolding of events demonstrated that this mode of thinking (on the part of the Jewish population) was incorrect. The Germans planned a full annihilation of both the peaceful and the extreme Jews, with no distinction. Alter Dvoretsky could foresee these preparations.

He was well-known in public affairs, active in Poalei Zion in Zhetel and in Vilna, and active as a teacher to the youth. In the Zhetel ghetto he was elected to the *Judenrat* [the Jewish Council]. It was not easy to function in this task and to maintain a moral lifestyle. As is known, the Germans would undertake their despicable deeds with the assistance of the *Judenrat*; however, Alter Dvoretsky took advantage of his position on the *Judenrat* in order to organize the youth for revolt and armed struggle.

In this work, he was assisted by the youth from among the refugees in the Zhetel ghetto. These young men, who had been exiled from their homes and who had lost their families [as well as] all of their possessions, discovered together a readiness to engage in resistance activity.

In his organization of the Jewish police in the Zhetel ghetto, Alter Dvoretsky, enlisted his supporters into its ranks. This enabled him to smuggle arms into the ghetto. With their assistance and with the assistance of former Soviet officers who had found shelter in surrounding villages, Dvoretsky managed to acquire arms. He received them in the cemetery and with the help of the Jewish police he hid them in an abandoned building.

Alter Dvoretsky also put together a plan in the event of liquidation (of the ghetto). For this purpose he divided the underground group into thirds and assigned each with special tasks. One third was supposed to set fire to the sawmill of Leib Kaplinski, the second—to the flourmill of Tchernikvitz. The rest were assigned to take control of the home of the head of the German police and the machine gun in the labor office.

The purpose of these actions was to arouse panic and chaos among the Germans and thus enable the youth to flee to the forests. This plan was never put into action. The transfer of Jews to the ghetto was not accompanied by an extermination action.

In the same period, Alter Dvoretsky made contact with a former Soviet officer, Vaniah. On the 26th of April, 1942 Vaniah met with members of the Zhetel underground and offered them weapons. This offer aroused suspicions. Abraham Alpert, the commander of the police in the ghetto, recommended not to hold the meeting (to acquire arms). Alter Dvoretsky also agreed with this assessment. However, a portion of the youth, chief among them Shalom Fiolon, decided that there was no danger in holding a meeting with Vaniah.

Just before evening, Shalom Fiolon snuck through the Zhetel ghetto fence and came to the meeting place. Vaniah was already waiting there for him and offered him a firearm. At this moment, they were set upon by police officers. Shalom Fiolon tried to shoot at them but his gun misfired.

The police subjected Shalom Fiolon to intense torture, but he did not reveal the secrets of the underground. In a note that was smuggled into the ghetto written in his blood he wrote: 'Comrades, do not be afraid, I will not betray you, continue the resistance and avenge my spilled blood!'

The members of the ghetto underground were not certain that Shalom Fiolon would be able to withstand the torture and they decided to flee to the forest. On the 28th of April Alter Dvoretsky, along with his assistants: Yonah Medbetsky, Eliezer Vinersky, and Pesach Finkelstein left the ghetto and headed for the forest.

In the forest, Alter Dvoretsky established contact with Christian partisans. He proposed to them an attack on Zhetel, in order to save the ghetto, but the Christian partisans were not convinced (of the necessity of such a move). The [Christian] partisans' principle aims in this time period were to obtain food and drink and to avoid contact with the Germans. [Moreover], they did not feel any particular affinity towards the Jews. The partisans invited Dvoretsky to a meeting

to discuss his bold plan. On the way back from the meeting, Alter Dvoretsky and Moshe Pozdonsky were attacked by a group of these partisans. In the fight that ensued they were both killed, defending the honor of Israel. Their grave is located in a wood near Podivorka. May their memory be honored!"
  –Shalom Gerling, www.ushmm.org

[8] **Partisans** "Some Jews who managed to escape from ghettos and camps formed their own fighting units. These fighters, or partisans, were concentrated in densely wooded areas. A large group of partisans in occupied Soviet territory hid in a forest near the Lithuanian capital of Vilna. They were able to derail hundreds of trains and kill over 3,000 German soldiers.

  Life as a partisan in the forest was difficult. People had to move from place to place to avoid discovery, raid farmers' food supplies to eat, and try to survive the winter in flimsy shelters built from logs and branches. In some places, partisans received assistance from local villagers, but more often they could not count on help, partly because of widespread antisemitism, partly because of people's fears of being severely punished for helping. The partisans lived in constant danger of local informers revealing their whereabouts to the Germans."—www.ushmm.org

[9] **The value of leather** Most of us are used to having many pairs of shoes because for us they are relatively cheap. However, in the early and mid twentieth-century, shoes and boots were very expensive and, thus, very valuable, especially boots. Leather was very expensive. That is the reason that earlier Mojshe's mother had given him a new pair of shoes; this was like money (see note 6). That is why a person could be killed for his pair of leather boots. People would trade the boots and shoes for food and/or booze.

[10] **Revenge** "As one partisan concedes—and this is amply borne out in other accounts . . ., 'The need for revenge was uppermost in the thoughts and blood of every Jewish partisan.' ('Indeed, . . . , seeking revenge, often to fulfill the dying wishes of one's family to avenge their deaths, is a *leitmotif* that permeates Holocaust memoirs'" [Aron, *Fallen Leaves*, 147]).—Paul, Mark. *A Tangled Web*. Part III:15.

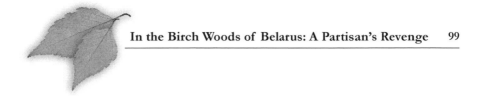

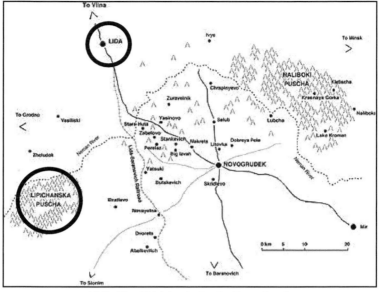

Naliboki and Lipichanska Puscha (Dense forest)
novogrudek.co.uk

[11] The Battle of Stalingrad The battle and "the bitter siege that had been sustained in and around that Russian city from August of 1942 to February of 1943. The defeat of the German Sixth Army at Stalingrad not only dealt a crippling blow to Hitler's campaign in the East but also marked the strategic turning point of the Second World War, and has come to be recognized as one of the greatest military debacles of all time. Over the years, the terrible fighting at Stalingrad has also come to symbolize the senseless sacrifice of human life to individual hubris and political whim.

In mid-November of 1942, a surprise pincer attack by two Russian armies cut off the German Sixth Army, which was then locked in a bloody struggle for the city of Stalingrad. Trapped in a *Kessel*, or cauldron, an egg-shaped line of defense thirty miles wide and twenty miles deep, the Sixth Army, which was under the command of General Friedrich Paulus, was ordered by Hitler to hold its ground rather than retreat west to join the vanguard of the German forces.

In a matter of two months, from late November of 1942 until the end of January of 1943, a quarter of a million German soldiers, a thousand German panzers, eighteen hundred pieces of artillery, an entire air force of transport

planes, and untold quantities of military supplies were obliterated by the combined forces of the Soviet Army and the Russian winter."
—www.writing.upenn.edu
Starvation, disease, and despair also contributed to the German defeat.
—militaryhistoryonline.com

[12] **N.K.V.D**. "The *Narodnyi Komissariat Vnutrennikh Del* (or NKVD) (Russian: НКВД, People's Commissariat for Internal Affairs) was a government agency that handled a number of the Soviet Union's affairs of state. The NKVD is best known as the secret agency of the Soviet Union. On February 3, 1941, the Special Sections of the NKVD (responsible for counter-intelligence in the military) became part of the Army and Navy (RKKA and RKKF, respectively). The GUGB was removed from the NKVD and renamed the NKGB. Following the outbreak of World War II, the NKVD and NKGB were reunited on July 20, 1941 and counter-intelligence was returned to the NKVD in January 1942. In April 1943 it was again transferred to the Narkomat of Defence and Narkomat of the Navy, becoming SMERSH (from *Smert' Shpionam* or "Death to Spies"); at the same time, the NKVD was again separated from the NKGB. . . . .

In 1946, the NKVD was renamed the MVD and the NKGB was renamed the MGB. Following yet another merger with the MVD in 1953, the Checkist forces were finally removed from the MVD in 1954 to finally become the KGB."–en.wikipedia.org

[13] **Vilna** "In July 1944 the Polish Home Army—Vilna Uprising—and then the Red Army seized Vilnius, which was shortly afterwards incorporated into the Soviet Union and made the capital of the newly created Lithuanian SSR. Immediately after World War II, the Soviet government decided to expel the Polish population from Lithuania and Belarus during the so-called repatriation. These events, coupled with the migration of the Lithuanian rural population and Russians from other Soviet republics during the post-war years, resulted in a complete change of the city's demographics, culture, and tradition."
—en/wikipedia.org/wiki/vilnius

 **Member Pin**

[14] **Komsomol** (Комсомол) "a syllabic abbreviation word, from the Russian *Kommunisticheskiy Soyuz Molodiozhi* (Коммунистический союз молодёжи), or "Communist Union of Youth". The organization was established on October 29, 1918. Since 1922 the full official name of it was *Vsesoyuzny Leninskiy Kommunisticheskiy Soyuz Molodyozhi* (VLKSM) (Russian: Всесоюзный Ленинский Коммунистический Союз Молодёжи (ВЛКСМ); English: All-Union Leninist Young Communist League).

Komsomol served as the youth wing of the Communist Party of the Soviet Union (CPSU), the youngest members being fourteen years old, the upper limit for an age of rank and file being 28, while *Komsomol* functionaries could be older. Younger children could join the allied Pioneers organisation.

Komsomol had little direct influence on the Communist Party, and on the government of the Soviet Union. But *Komsomol* played an important role as a mechanism for teaching the values of the CPSU in the young, and as an organ for introducing the young to the political domain. Along with these purposes, the organisation served as a highly mobile pool of labour and political activism, with the ability to move to areas of high-priority at short notice. Active members received privileges and preferences in promotion." —en.wikipedia.org

[15] **Vladivostok** in the Russian Far East, on the coast of the Sea of Japan and near both the Chinese and Korean borders. "Home base of the Russian Pacific Fleet, the city was closed to all non-Soviets from 1958 until 1991. In the early part of the 20th century, Russians were actually outnumbered by Chinese in Vladivostok, and during the years following the Revolution, there were large Japanese and US populations. The US maintained a consulate in Vladivostok until 1948.

In the 1930s mass repressions began in the Soviet Union, and a transit camp for political prisoners carried from the Western regions of Russia to Kolyma, Siberia, was opened in Vladivostok. The prisoners arrived by trains and later were transported on prison ships, in terrible conditions. The prisoners, at first Soviet, after 1939 from Eastern Europe, and after the end of the World War II the Japanese POWs, constituted a considerable part of the labor force that built factories, ports, and cities in the Far East from 1930 through 1940. Here Russia's strategic defense batteries were located during World War II, discouraging a Japanese invasion. There have been ammunition dumps and command centers in the taiga near Vladivostok since the 1930s, as well as a network of underground tunnels running many kilometers." —www.infoplease.com

Focal Point and World Media

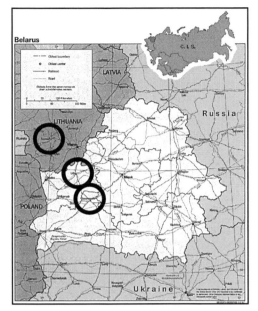

[16] Baranovicia and Lida, Belarus, and Kovno (Kaunas), Lithuania

[17] Lida, Belarus

jewishgen.org/Belarus

[18] **Kovno, Lithuania**. See map under note 16. "Between the World Wars industry prospered in Kovno (Kaunas), as it was the largest city in Lithuania. In 1940 it was annexed by the Soviet Union into the Lithuanian SSR. The Jewish population of Kovno, 37,000 people, was attacked by anti-Communist Lithuanian

partisans, killing 3,800 people (see the Jager Report), some of these massacres were even filmed. Under German occupation 1941-1944 most of the remaining Jewish population was confined in the Kaunas Ghetto (also known as the Kauen concentration camp), and many were shot at the Ninth Fort. Only 3,000 or so Jews survived the war." —en.wikipedia.org

[19] **White Russian** The designation "White" has several interpretations. It was historically applied to different regions in Eastern Europe, most often to the region that roughly corresponds to the present-day Belarus. Many languages today continue to use this obsolete name when referring to Belarus.

In addition, it stood in contradistinction to the Reds—the revolutionary Red Army who supported the Soviets and Communism. Second, the word "white" had monarchist associations: historically each Russian Tsar was solemnly called the white tsar. Third, the word "white" was often associated with freedom, as in the Domostroi book where free land is called "white land."

Strictly speaking, no monolithic "White Army" existed; lacking central coordination, the White forces were never more than a loose confederation of counter-revolutionary forces. The most common goal of the white forces was to overthrow the Bolshevik government in favor of the Russian Constituent Assembly, a democratically elected body which was to determine the future political fate of Russia.

The officers who made up the core of the armies upheld a variety of political orientations, monarchist, republican democratic, occasionally supporters of the social revolutionary, and any other political orientation opposed to the October Revolution and the Bolsheviks. A majority of them believed in a united Russia (were opposed to nationalist separatism) and tended to gravitate towards a monarchy or a conservative republican government. Those of more left wing (i.e. leftist SR, Menshevik) or nationalistically separatist orientations were known occasionally to switch sides.

Bolshevik and Menshevik The two factions were originally known as "hard" (Lenin's supporters) and "soft" (Martov's supporters). Soon, however, the terminology changed to "Bolsheviks" and "Mensheviks," from the Russian "bolshinstvo" (majority) and "menshinstvo" (minority), based on the fact that Lenin's supporters narrowly defeated Martov's supporters on the question of party membership. Neither Lenin nor Martov had a firm majority throughout the Congress as delegates left or switched sides. At the end, the Congress was evenly

split between the two factions.

Lenin advocated limiting party membership to a small core of professional revolutionaries, leaving sympathizers outside the party, and instituting a system of centralized control known as the democratic centralist model. Julius Martov, until then a close friend and colleague of Lenin's, agreed with him that the core of the party should consist of professional revolutionaries, but argued that party membership should be open to sympathizers, revolutionary workers and other fellow travellers.

[20] *Brichah* (Hebrew: flight, escape), the name given to the post World War II organization that organized illegal emigration from Eastern Europe into the Allied-occupied zones and Palestine and Israel. Zionists smuggled about 150,000 Jews across the borders, moving them into displaced persons camps in Germany, Austria, and Italy."Trouble in Eastern Europe in 1946 more than doubled the number of displaced persons. At the beginning of the war, about 150,000 Polish Jews escaped to the Soviet Union. In 1946 these Jews began being repatriated to Poland. There were reasons enough for Jews not to want to remain in Poland but one incident in particular convinced them to emigrate. On July 4, 1946, there was a pogrom against the Jews of Kielce and 41 people were killed and 60 were seriously injured. By the winter of 1946/1947, there were about a quarter of a million displaced persons (DPs) in Europe.

Truman agreed to loosen immigration laws in the United States and brought thousands of DPs into America. The priority immigrants were orphaned children. Over the course of 1946 to 1950, over 100,000 Jews migrated to the United States." —geography.about.com/od/populationgeography/a/displacedjews

[21] **Displaced Persons' Camp** (DP Camps) "A displaced persons camp is in principle any temporary facility for displaced persons but in common usage refers to camps for individuals displaced as a result of World War II, particularly refugees from Eastern Europe.

Combat operations, ethnic cleansing, genocide, secondary political conflicts, economic distress, and general fear resulted in millions of people being uprooted from their original homes in the course of World War II, becoming displaced. Estimates for the number of displaced persons varies from 11 million to as many as 20 million.

When the war ended, these people found themselves in unfamiliar places facing an uncertain future. Allied military and civilian authorities faced considerable challenges in resolving the problem of displaced persons.

For one thing, the reasons for their displacement varied considerably. For purposes of classification, the Supreme Headquarters Allied Expeditionary Force classified them into the categories of: evacuees, war or political refugees, political prisoners, forced or voluntary workers, Todt workers, former forces under German command, deportees, civilian internees, ex-prisoners of war, and stateless persons.

In addition, the origins of these people varied considerably. In addition to every country that had been invaded and/or occupied by German forces, many came from areas that had changed sovereignty in the course of the war, or where they had been refugees to begin with. Although the situation of many of the DPs could be resolved by simply moving them to their original homes, good solutions were elusive for a large minority.

Establishing a system for resolving displacement

The original plan for those displaced as a result of World War II was to repatriate them to their countries of origin as quickly as possible. Depending on sectors occupied in Austria and Germany, American, French, British, or Soviet forces tended to the immediate needs of the refugees and set in motion plans for repatriation. (Estimates for displaced persons do not typically include several million ethnic Germans in Eastern Europe who were expelled and repatriated in Germany. See German exodus from Eastern Europe.)

In the months and sometimes years following the end of the war, displaced persons typically reported to military personnel who attended to their immediate needs. Nearly all of them were malnourished, a great number were ill, and some were dying. Shelter was often improvised, and there were many instances of military personnel sharing from their own supplies of food, medicine, clothing, etc., to help the refugees. In a matter of weeks, there was a more or less formalized infrastructure for taking in, registering, treating, classifying, sorting, and transporting displaced persons.

On October 1, 1945 the United Nations Relief and Rehabilitation Administration (UNRRA) took responsibility for the administration of displaced persons in Europe, though military authorities continued to play a role for several years to come." –www.wikipedia.com

[22] **UNRRA** Representatives of 44 Allied nations met in Washington, D.C., and Atlantic City in November 1943. They set up the United Nations Relief and Rehabilitation Administration (UNRRA) to provide relief to areas liberated from Axis powers after World War II. UNRRA provided billions of US dollars of rehabilitation aid, and helped about 8 million refugees. It ceased operations in the DP camps of Europe in 1947, and in Asia in 1949, upon which it ceased to exist. Its functions were transferred to several UN agencies, including the International Refugee Organization. —Britannica online and en.wikipedia.org

[23] **Steyr** a town (population 39,495 as of 2001) in the Austrian federal state of Upper Austria, located at the confluence of the Rivers Steyr and Enns. "A major producer of arms and vehicles during the Second World War, Steyr became a target of Allied bombing raids that tried to knock out its factories. Much of the town was badly damaged, but the factories continued to function until near the end of the war. The city was a meeting point in May 1945, when units of the 5th Guards Airborne of the Red Army and black troops of the US 761st Tank Battalion along with the 71st Infantry Division contacted each other on the bridge over the Enns River. The city continued to be occupied—divided, like Berlin—by Soviet and American troops until 1955 when Austria was declared a neutral country and the occupiers left." —en.wikipedia.org

[24] **Soap** The story about Nazis making soap from Jewish bodies is one that has circulated for many years, especially among Holocaust survivors but also in the general population. However, recent articles, for example in *Ha'Aretz*, as well as the statements of Holocaust scholars discount this. Yehuda Bauer, distinguished Holocaust scholar and author, has said, "The story was spread as part of the Nazi campaign of psychological sadism, and very many Jews believed it in the past, and continue to believe it in the present. A type of soap that was produced by the Germans during the war was (and still is) considered to be made of human fat, and has the inscription R.I.F., which Jews erroneously interpreted as *Rein Juedisches Fett* (Pure Jewish Fat). But *Juedisch* is spelt with a "J" not with an "I," and the letters actually mean *Rheinlaendische Industrie Fettherstellung* (Rhineland Industrial Production). The Nazis did try to make fat from corpses, in early 1945, at an experimental station near Gdansk, out of the bodies of Polish slave laborers (not Jews). However, no industrial production was achieved, and the Soviets occupied the area in February 1945. The material was produced at the

Nuremberg Trials. Had there been a Nazi industrial production of human fat, they would not have needed an experimental station." July 10, 2006, email from Yehuda Bauer. Michael Berenbaum, author of the *World Must Know*, concurs.

Sidney Simon, who heard and believed these stories, buried the soap he found in the store in Steyr out of respect for the Jewish victims he believed this soap came from. The American MPs as well as the rabbis also believed the story. Because of all the atrocities that they had witnessed, Holocaust survivors believed the soap story as well. As Yehuda Bauer has said, "Holocaust survivors were prepared to believe any horror stories about their persecutors."

[25] **Organization for Rehabilitation through Training (ORT)** Displaced Person Camp Vocational Training: "During 1946 it became increasingly evident that Jews who had been deprived of all opportunities to acquire new skills or to use the abilities they once possessed were urgently in need of vocational training, not only for the economic advantage resulting from this type of instruction, but also for the recognized therapeutic value inherent in this training. In 1946 nearly 42,000 men and women were enrolled in Joint Distribution Committee projects, where their instruction ranged from short-term experience on a farm or in a machine shop to more intensive courses in preparation for a life of economic independence." —www.jewishlibrary.org

[26] ***Eretz Israel*** "The Land of Israel (Hebrew: לארשי ץרא *Eretz Yisrael*) is a concept in Jewish and Christian thought concerning the area today most closely associated with the State of Israel, throughout its history, from Biblical times to the present day.

During the British Mandate of Palestine, the name *Eretz Yisrael* (abbreviated י"א *Aleph-Yod*), was part of the official name of the territory, when written in Hebrew. That name was (י"א הניתשלפ). The government of the British Mandate of Palestine wanted the name to be הניתשלפ (*Palestina*) while the *Yishuv* wanted לארשי ץרא (*Eretz Yisrael*). The compromise eventually achieved was that the initials י"א would be written in brackets whenever הניתשלפ is written. Consequently, in 20th century political usage, the term 'Land of Israel' usually denotes only those parts of the land which came under the British mandate, that is, the land currently controlled by the State of Israel, the West Bank, and the Gaza Strip, and sometimes also Transjordan (now the Kingdom of Jordan)."

[27] ***Haganah*** "The underground military organization of the *Yishuv [Jewish community]* in *Eretz Yisrael* from 1920 to 1948. The Arab riots in 1920 and 1921 (see also *Tel Hai*) strengthened the view that it was impossible to depend upon the British authorities and that the *Yishuv* needed to create an independent defense force completely free of foreign authority. In June 1920, the *Haganah* was founded.

During the first nine years of its existence, the *Haganah* was a loose organization of local defense groups in the large towns and in several of the settlements. The Arab riots in 1929 brought about a complete change in the *Haganah's* status.

- It became a large organization encompassing nearly all the youth and adults in the settlements, as well as several thousand members from each of the cities.
- It initiated a comprehensive training program for its members, ran officers' training courses.
- Established central arms depots into which a continuous stream of light arms flowed from Europe.
- Simultaneously, the basis was laid for the underground production of arms.

Haganah branches were established at Jewish DP (displaced persons) camps in Europe and *Haganah* members accompanied the 'illegal' immigrant boats. In the spring of 1947, David Ben-Gurion took it upon himself to direct the general policy of the *Haganah*, especially in preparation for impending Arab attack. On May 26 1948, the Provisional Government of Israel decided to transform the *Haganah* into the regular army of the State, to be '*Zeva Haganah Le-Yisrael*'" —The Israel Defense Forces.

[28] **British Mandate in Palestine** "In June 1922 the League of Nations passed the Palestine Mandate. The Palestine Mandate was an explicit document regarding Britain's responsibilities and powers of administration in Palestine including 'secur[ing] the establishment of the Jewish national home,' and 'safeguarding the civil and religious rights of all the inhabitants of Palestine.'

The document defining Britain's obligations as Mandate power copied the text of the Balfour Declaration concerning the establishment of a Jewish homeland:

His Majesty's Government view with favour the establishment in Palestine of a national home for the Jewish

people, and will use their best endeavours to facilitate the achievement of this object, it being clearly understood that nothing shall be done which may prejudice the civil and religious rights of existing non-Jewish communities in Palestine, or the rights and political status enjoyed by Jews in any other country.

Many articles of the document specified actions in support of Jewish immigration and political status. However, it was also stated that in the large, mostly arid, territory to the east of the Jordan River, then called Transjordan, Britain could 'postpone or withhold' application of the provisions dealing with the 'Jewish National Home.'

The Holocaust had a major effect on the situation in Palestine. During the war, the British forbade entry into Palestine of European Jews escaping Nazi persecution, placing them in detention camps or deporting them to places such as Mauritius. Avraham Stern, the leader of the Jewish Lehi, whose will to fight the British was so strong he offered to fight on the Nazi side, and other Zionists, tried to convince the Nazis to continue seeing emigration from Europe as the 'solution' for their 'Jewish problem,' but the Nazis gradually abandoned this idea in favor of containment and physical extermination.

Starting in 1939, the Zionists organized an illegal immigration effort, known as *Aliya Beth*, conducted by '*Hamossad Le'aliyah Bet*,' that rescued tens of thousands of European Jews from the Nazis by shipping them to Palestine in rickety boats. Many of these boats were intercepted. The last immigrant boat to try to enter Palestine during the war was the *Struma*, torpedoed in the Black Sea by a Soviet submarine in February 1942. The boat sank with the loss of nearly 800 lives. Illegal immigration resumed after WW II.

Following the war, 250,000 Jewish refugees were stranded in displaced persons (DP) camps in Europe. Despite the pressure of world opinion, in particular the repeated requests of US President Harry S. Truman and the recommendations of the Anglo-American Committee of Inquiry, the British refused to lift the ban on immigration and admit 100,000 displaced persons to Palestine. The Jewish underground forces then united and carried out several attacks against the British. In 1946, the Irgun blew up the King David Hotel in Jerusalem, the headquarters of the British administration, killing 92 people.

Because the situation was quickly spiraling out of hand, the British announced their desire to terminate their mandate and to withdraw by May 1948."
—en.wikipedia.org

A passenger poses on the deck of the *Marine Flasher*
just before its departure from the port of Bremerhaven. –www.ushmm.org

[29] USS *Marine Flasher* "In May 1946, the *Marine Flasher* transported 867 European DPs to the U.S., the first contingent to be admitted under President Truman's December 1945 directive expediting the immigration of displaced persons to the U.S. Four hundred and fifty of these new immigrants were assisted by the American Joint Distribution Committee (the Joint). The *Marine Flasher* continued transporting displaced persons after 1946." –www.ushmm.org

Marine Flasher/Long Beach 1945

"This was the *Marine Flasher*. One of a class of 15 ships designated C4-S-A3, 12,420 gross tons, length 523ft x beam 71.2ft, one funnel engines aft, single screw, speed 17 knots. Accommodation was for 3,800 troops. Built by Kaiser Shipyard, Vancouver, Washington, she was launched for the US Maritime Commission 16th May 1945. Chartered to the United States Lines in 1946 and fitted with accommodation for 914 tourist class passengers, she started her first New York-Havre voyage on 25 May 1946. In September1949 she was returned to the USMC.

She was then laid up until 1966, when she was sold to Litton Industries Leasing Corp, Wilmington, Delaware, and rebuilt as the container ship *Long Beach*, 17,814 gross tons, length 684ft x beam 78.1ft. 1975 sold to Reynolds Leasing Corp. In 1988 she grounded at San Juan becoming a constructive total loss. [Great Passenger Ships of the World by Arnold Kludas, vol.4]." –www.shipslist.com

[30] **Scrap Metal** "a term used to describe the recycling of metal. Old, unwanted metal such as vehicles, building supplies, and surplus materials, are taken to a scrapyard, where they are processed for later melting into new products.

A scrapyard (also known as Breakers), depending on your location, may allow you to browse their lot and purchase items before they are sent to the smelters although many scrap yards that deal in large quantities of scrap usually do not, often selling entire units such as engines or machinery by weight with no regard to their functional status. You are typically required to supply all your own tools and labor to extract parts, and some scrapyards may require you to first waive liability for personal injury before entering. Many scrapyards also sell bulk metals (stainless steel, etc) by weight, often at prices substantially below the retail purchasing costs of similar pieces, and can be a gold mine if they have what you need for a project — the proverbial 'One man's trash is another man's treasure.'

In contrast to a wreckers, scrapyards typically sell everything by weight, rather than by item. To the scrapyard, the primary value of the scrap is what the smelter will give them for it, rather than the value of whatever shape the metal may be in. An auto wrecker, on the other hand, would price the exact same scrap based on what the item does, regardless of what it weighs. Typically, if a wrecker can not sell something above the value of the metal in it, they would then take it to the scrapyard and sell it by weight. Equipment containing parts of various metals can often be purchased at a price below that of either of the metals, due to saving the scrapyard the labor of separating the metals before shipping them to be recycled. As an example, a scrapyard in Arcata, California sells automobile engines for $0.25 per pound, while aluminum, of which the engine is mostly made, sells for $1.25 per pound." —en.wikipedia.com/scrap_metal

Sidney had learned about metals in the DP camps from ORT training. He worked briefly in a scrap metal yard before he started his own scrap metal business, collecting metals not for weight but for their value.

[31] **Chicken Farms** Many Holocaust survivors settled in South Jersey, buying and operating chicken farms. For these farms they did not need language skills.

Sidney and Rosalie and two of their children lived for a time on a chicken farm that Sidney had bought and operated with his father and brother, Richard.

See also McLoughlin, Maryann. "The Third Wave: Holocaust Survivors and South Jersey Farms." In *Holocaust Survivors of South Jersey: Portraits of Resilience.*

[32] **Bader Field Airport** also known as Atlantic City Municipal Airport, was a general aviation airport located in Atlantic City, New Jersey, approximately one mile from the terminus of U.S. Route 40 and U.S. Route 322. The airport, which opened in 1910, covered 143 acres and had two runways. The first known usage of the term "air-port" appeared in a newspaper article in 1919, in reference to Bader Field. Bader Field was the founding location of the Civil Air Patrol in 1941. This airport permanently closed on September 30, 2006.—en.wikipedia.com

[33] **Candling Eggs** To examine (an egg) for freshness or fertility by holding it before a bright light. –www.freedictionary.com *"Candling* is so named because in days gone by an egg was held up in front of a candle to see inside. Today, candling is more likely to be accomplished electrically, with the eggs moving and rotating on rollers over high-intensity lights." --www.epicurious.com/cooking

[34] **Post-Partum Depression** "Depression after pregnancy is called postpartum depression or peripartum depression. After pregnancy, hormonal changes in a woman's body may trigger symptoms of depression. During pregnancy, the amount of two female hormones, estrogen and progesterone, in a woman's body increases greatly. In the first 24 hours after childbirth, the amount of these hormones rapidly drops back down to their normal non-pregnant levels. Researchers think the fast change in hormone levels may lead to depression.

Postpartum depression can happen anytime within the first year after childbirth. A woman may have a number of symptoms such as sadness, lack of energy, trouble concentrating, anxiety, and feelings of guilt and worthlessness. The difference between postpartum depression and the baby blues is that postpartum depression often affects a woman's well-being and keeps her from functioning well for a longer period of time. Postpartum depression needs to be treated by a doctor."—w ww.4women.gov/FAQ/postpartum

[35] **Rosalie Lebovic Simon** Rosalie is also a Holocaust survivor, a survivor of Auschwitz.

The "Ike Jacket"

[36] **Eisenhower Jacket** The "Ike Jacket" During World War II, the popular image of General Eisenhower depicts him wearing a well tailored, short-waisted, smart-looking jacket, designated officially as the "Wool Field Jacket, M-1944." To the troops it was known as the ETO (European Theater of Operations) Jacket, or even more popularly as the "Ike Jacket."
    —www.eisenhowerarchives.gov

Photographs

Sidney is the little boy. He is with Meyer's family. Meyer is Sidney's father's brother. Sidney's Hebrew teacher, Hirsche Leizer, is in the back row the second one from the right - Pre World War II.

Elie Chaym, Jankel (in the partisans), and Moishe, Sidney's brother.

The bridge over the River Neman.

The scaffolding of the bridge where partisans hid when they set fire to the bridge over the Neman.

Sidney in his Soviet uniform post-World War II.

Sidney in Branau, Austria, at the Braunau DP Camp theatre group - 1946.

Sidney in the Braunau DP Camp theatre group—playing the accordion - 1946.

Sidney in the DP camp, in ORT, learning to repair cars as part of chauffeur training. This car was made from parts found in scrap yards - 1946.

Burying soap in the Jewish Cemetery at Steyr (see Chapter 24).

Burying soap in the Jewish Cemetery at Steyr (see Chapter 24).

Burying soap in the Jewish Cemetery at Steyr (see Chapter 24).

In Baltimore, Maryland, after immigration, L to R: Friend of Morton's, Tante Clara, Morton (Joe's son), and Uncle Joe.

Czerna and Samuel, Sidney's mother and father in the United States.

Sidney retrieving scrap metal from Meyerhof's.

Sidney (R) and his brother, Richard (L), at the Wailing Wall in Jerusalem, Israel.

Sidney, with his sisters, Ida and Katie, and his brother, Richard.

Mitchell, William, and Ruthie.

Mitchell—Sidney and Rosalie's older son.

Ruthie—Sidney and Rosalie's daughter.

William—Sidney and Rosalie's younger son.

Sidney at his office in McKee City with surplus cars and trucks.

Sidney with Moshe Dayan, Minister of Defense of Israel.

Sidney and Ruthie with Moshe Dayan and his associate in Israel.

Sidney speaking in Israel.

Rosalie, Sidney, Richard, Betty, Shunek, and Ida.   Rosalie and Sidney.

Sidney's 60th Birthday, Sidney and Rosalie.

Sidney and Rosalie, signing the
"Scroll of Remembrance"
- United States Holocaust Memorial Museum
in Washington, D.C.

William, Debbie, Mitchell, Ruthie-second row; Rosalie and Sidney, first row.

Sidney in Acapulco, with his catch—a 210 pound Marlin.

Sidney at graduation from the Atlantic County Institute of Technology.

Sidney and his grandson Erik.

Erik and Sidney.

Ruthie and Erik

Erik.

Ruthie and Erik.

Mitchell and Debbie..

Rosalie, Jared, and Sidney.

Danny, Rosalie, and Matthew, Oceanside,
New York.

Daniel, Jared, Matthew.

Daniel, Debbie, Matthew, Mitchell, and Jared.

Daniel, Jared, Matthew.

Jared, Daniel, Matthew—first row;
Sidney, Erik, Rosalie—second row.

Mitchell and Debbie

William.

William and Sidney.

William and Jody.

William and Jody's wedding—Mitchell, Debbie, Sidney, Rosalie, William, Jody, Matthew, Jared, Daniel, Ruthie, and Erik in front.

Jody and William
with Raegan Aliya.

Raegan Aliya, held up by William.

Raegan Aliya, 1 1/2 years.

William and Jody.

Belitze, 1999: Erica, Charlotte, Rosalie, Betty, Richard, Valerie, Renee, Marsha; in the front: William.

Villagers greeting the group of forty-two from the United States and Israel with *challah* (bread), the traditional symbol of welcome, Belitze, Belarus, 1999.

Sidney speaking with a group of villagers, Belitze, Belarus, 1999.

Sidney with village woman, Belitze, Belarus, 1999. Behind is the Jewish Cemetery.

Richard and Betty Simon next to
memorial in Belitze, Belarus, 1999.

L to R: Sidney and Richard with village woman,
Belitze, Belarus, 1999.

L to R: Richard and Sidney at memorial to
murdered Jews, Belitze, Belarus, 1999.

Rosalie, Sidney, and William at memorial to
murdered Jews, Belitze, Belarus, 1999.

Right corner: Sidney and Rosalie in front of memorial in Belitze, Belarus, 1999, includes Richard and Betty Simon and cousins.

Charlotte (Katie's daughter), Marsha (Richard's daughter), Lilly (Ida's daughter) in Belitze, Belarus, 1999.

Sidney Simon standing beside the memorial to 2130 Jews murdered on May 19, 1942, and buried in a mass grave, Belitze, 1999. Inscription on stone reads as follows: "Here lies the esteemed sage, Rabbi Israel Meyr, better known as Hafetz Haim. He was a world famous rabbi, author, teacher, and Jewish community leader of the region."

Memorial to Jews murdered on December 28, 1942, and buried in a mass grave, Belitze, Belarus, 1999.

Mr. Sheshko. The mother and the two sons are not pictured (*Book of Belitzah*. Ed. L. Losh. Tel Aviv: 1968).

Sheshko sisters. The mother and the two sons are not pictured (*Book of Belitzah*. Ed. L. Losh. Tel Aviv: 1968).

Memorial to Jews murdered and buried in a mass grave, Belitze, Belarus.

Kulesh and Sidney talking, 1999.

Family celebrating their trip to Belitze, Belarus, 1999: on the right seated— R to L: Sidney and Rosalie.

Family celebrating the trip to Belitze, Belarus, 1999: on the right, leaning over, is William— Sidney and Rosalie's younger son.

Sidney's 80th Birthday: Standing, L to R: Danny, Debbie, Mitchell, Jared, Alicia, Matthew, Rosalie; Seated, L to R: William, Jody, Sidney, and Ruthie.